BECOME A 21ST CENTURY ENTREPRENEUR

JJ Simmons

WWW.JJSIMMONS.ORG

Copyright © 2018 by **JJ Simmons**

All rights reserved. No part of this book may be used or reproduced by any means, graphic, elec- tronic, or mechanical, including photocopying, recording, taping or by any information storage retrieval system without the written permission of the publisher except in the case of brief quotations embodied in critical articles and reviews.

JJ Simmons/Thou Shall Prosper TV
Houston, Texas
www.jjsimmons.org

Scripture quotations marked (NKJV) are taken from the New King James Version®. Copyright © 1982 by Thomas Nelson. Used by permission. All rights reserved.

Scripture quotations marked (NIV) are taken from the Holy Bible, New International Version®, NIV®. Copyright © 1973, 1978, 1984, 2011 by Biblica, Inc.™ Used by permission of Zondervan. All rights reserved.

Become A 21st Century Entrepreneur/ JJ Simmons

ISBN-10: 1725741059
ISBN-13: 978-1725741058

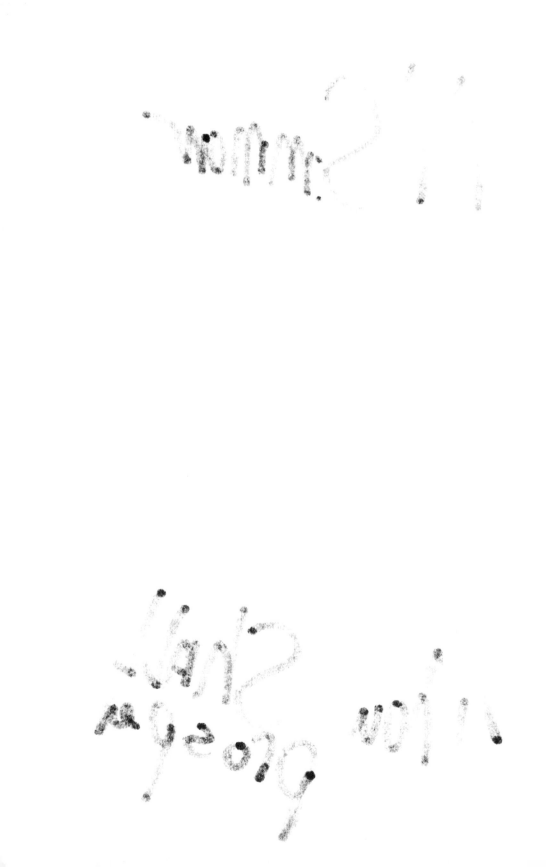

DEDICATION

This book is dedicated to my family: my wife Shawn Simmons the queen of my universe, my children, Zaria, Joel, Zoe, Christian, Jordan, and Lincoln. You guys are the reasons I have placed such a demand on my potential to become all that I have become and will continue to transform into as time progress.

To my beautiful Mother it was you who taught me to love and love with mercy.

You have been so sacrificial to me it's unbelievable what you have done for me these last 33 years of my life. To my beautiful sister Mandalee you are so beautiful and I know you want to have fun and enjoy life. My true desire and prayer for you is that you will seek God and discover your purpose and how you will change the world and leave your mark in this world. The two most important days in a person's life is the day they were born, and the day they discover why they were born.

I love you and appreciate every last one of you.

This book is also dedicated to every entrepreneur out here who is burning with passion every single day for your businesses to blow up like you know they should. I wrote this book for you because inside of books is where I found the treasures of life that I discovered when I was extremely hungry to find answers and solutions in my life.

It's my prayer that inside of this book, you find multiple gems that are priceless and that will accelerate you to get to your future. It's my desire that this book will become like traveling on a jet from New Orleans to Alaska versus walking from New Orleans to Alaska; both will get you there, but the jet will get you there faster.

I also want to dedicate this book to my Pastor Jamail Johnson of the greatest Church in Houston Texas The Word Church. It's because of you I decided to be Great. In the fall of 2014 you preached the most life altering sermons I have ever heard in my life. My destiny was in that word and for that I will forever be grateful for you.

To Dr. Mike Murdock you imparted The hunger for the Wisdom of God in my life you taught that men only fail because of broken focus, you taught me that its two ways to get Wisdom people or pain, and if we don't get it through people that pain will schedule it for you. You taught me wisdom is a principal thing. You taught me sow into my future. You taught that until I ask a question my knowledge is accidental.

To Grant Cardone you taught me to never change the goal but to increase my level of activity, you taught me to be obsessed about my purpose, you taught to train daily in sales, you taught me to always have a target, you taught me sell or be sold. Its because of you I have taught my kids how to sell sale with skills not just personality. It's because of you that obsession has become my greatest gift. It was you who gave me permission to become a maniac, to proclaim my greatness, to make a big claim and so much more.

I wrote this book for you guys. I hope it truly helps.

TABLE OF CONTENTS

INTRODUCTION...1
Chapter 1:   Become a 21st
                  Century Entrepreneur..4
Chapter 2:   Become a Marketer..12
Chapter 3:   Become a Salesperson....................................18
Chapter 4:   Become a Technician......................................27
Chapter 5:   Become a Speaker..34
Chapter 6:   Become a Networker......................................41
Chapter 7:   Become a Self-Proclaimer..............................47
Chapter 8:   Become a Manager..55
Chapter 9:   Become a Negotiator......................................61
Chapter 10:   Become a Learner..68
Chapter 11:   Become an Obsessive Student.......................88
Chapter 12:   Become a Finisher..97
Chapter 13:   Become a Creator..102
Chapter 14:   Become an Opportunist...............................111
Chapter 15:   Become a Monster..116
Chapter 16:   Become a Non-Emotional Savage................121
CONCLUSION...130
ABOUT THE AUTHOR..131

INTRODUCTION

WHY I WROTE THIS BOOK

Between 2003-2005, I was a hip-hop artist in New Orleans really giving it all I had to one day blow up as an artist in the hip-hop industry. And I remember praying out loud, "God if you would just give me an opportunity to one day live off of my music career..." then Katrina happened. Now, having to leave, I'm in this brand new big city with so much possibility. I remember being in the incredible city and being inspired as I have never been before.

I remember meeting people who had their own businesses selling graphic design services, car washes, printing business, food trucks, etc., you name it, Houston had it. Then I remember one day making $200 selling our CDs on the street; I was blown away. I said to myself, "OMG, if I could do this every day, then I will never need to work a 9 to 5." Then before I knew it, I was doing it every day plus more. In life, location is everything. You could be the perfect person with an okay product and still make a fortune because the location is already conducive to your industry and you prosper.

Let me explain. They've seafood restaurant here in Houston that everyone is just crazy over. But to me, being from New Orleans, it's really average because in New Orleans, that product is normal. So because they are in Houston, they are making a fortune. But take that same restaurant and place it in New Orleans and they wouldn't make as much because that's common in New Orleans. So for me, I was the right person in the wrong location when I was in New Orleans. When I came to Houston and saw what was available and possible, my mind forever changed.

When I began to meet so many people in Houston that were full-time entrepreneurs, it affected me in a major way. I remember meeting an artist in Houston that was very average in his skill set but was making plenty of money. I was perplexed and really couldn't understand how these people were making so much money in their careers.

Back then, I didn't understand things like I do now. These guys had skill sets that equipped them to make money which had nothing to do with the skill sets to be rappers. I have seen average people become great, I have also seen potentially great people live with potential and never become great.

So, this is why I created this blueprint to teach you what I didn't know back then, which it is completely possible to BECOME someone. Basically, build a brand new you. You can identify what skill sets you need to become who you want to be and access what you want in order to access the future you.

I have met rappers who were incredible. I mean, extremely gifted, but they never made it out of their cities. I have met bakers that their pastries are incredible, but they only ended up selling to their family and close friends. I have met speakers who can't market, and marketers who can't sell to save their life.

In my honest opinion, I believe this is the most important book on entrepreneurship ever. Forget every other book that has been written, ever. So, I wrote this book to help and assist you to no longer lose any more time in your life because time is all you have left.

The skills you need to access your future require knowledge first, then after you attain the knowledge, that knowledge will assist you in how to activate that skill that you are in pursuit of.

CHAPTER 1

BECOME A 21ST CENTURY ENTREPRENEUR

One of the greatest things I have learned in my life is that I can become someone that I wasn't at first. I used to think that whatever gift or skill that I was born with was my limitation, and I couldn't participate and become even greater than what I had already possessed. That was really heartbreaking to me, and it created this belief in me that it was out of my control. This, in turn, put me in the position to never take control of my life and develop new disciplines to become a greater version of me.

Then one day I heard Dr. Mike Murdock say, "Everybody wants to be, but only a few are willing to become." I heard that, and that wisdom key planted a thought in my mind that I could become whatever I wanted to become if I was willing to become.

Let's look at the definition of become: qualified or accepted as; acquire the status of.

turn into, change into, be transformed into, be converted into

Now look at the word acquire.

Buy or obtain. Learn or develop (a skill, habit, or quality).

To become someone, you must acquire knowledge that's connected to the person you want to become. No one is born a lawyer, doctor, chef, speaker, dentist, etc., the only thing that makes these people earn the title that they have is that they acquired the knowledge that gave them the skills to practice whatever they are practicing.

Look at everyone today that you admire, they have knowledge that you don't have, and that's the great divide. However, the good news of this book is that you too can become that which they are, in your own time and according to the level of your hunger and discipline, to become that which your heart desires to become.

Look at the synonyms: Turn into, change into, be transformed into, be converted into. You have the potential, which means possibilities, to turn into, be transformed into, be converted into, etc.

The choice is truly yours. You can become a 21st Century Entrepreneur. Now, what exactly is a 21st Century Entrepreneur?

When I think of the term 21st Century Entrepreneur, I think of the entrepreneur that understands why Toys "R" Us went out of business after being so dominant for so many years. Television and radio are no longer the Gods of media because Spotify, Pandora, Podcasts, YouTube, and social media have taken so much money from them.

Now, when we want to market to our target audience, we don't even think of radio stations anymore. The 21st Century Entrepreneur laughs at the thought of radio and television as media outlets that we must respect and bow down to.

Quick Story: A few months ago, I was making a true push to market to my New Orleans audience. So, I found a guy that has 91.2k followers on Instagram and paid him a few $100 to post my content on his page once a week to be able to reach the people I'm trying to reach through him. And I actually gained followers from it and made a few sales from people recognizing me on the streets from his page.

In my mind, I would spend that money 20 times before I go to a radio station for multiple reasons:

1. Social media shows you the numbers.
2. The whole world is on their phone.
3. It means it's directly to the audience through their phone.

The 21st Century Entrepreneur understands what the 21st century consumer is interested in and what they are not interested in. The 21st century consumer is selfish with their time; they are more time-conscious than any consumer has been in the history of the world. The language that a 21st century consumer loves is the word speed.

So many thought leaders have made the statement that this generation is busier and moving at a faster pace than ever. That's true, and everybody is in a rush to get somewhere, and some are in a rush to get nowhere. However, Netflix won from that idea of us being in the rush because the 21st century consumer knows how to slow down for what he is interested in, not what somebody wants to slow them down for. The 21st century consumer hates television but is faithful at watching his favorite show on demand, why? Because he is selfish with his time; they don't invest in anything that they are not interested in.

The 21st century consumer investigates your business for weeks, maybe even months before they spend one dime with you. And the 21st Century Entrepreneur must understand this very important truth if they plan on thriving in this economy. The 21st Century Entrepreneur understands that the 21st century consumer is lazy but in a rush at the same time. What do I mean?

The 21st Century Entrepreneur needs to understand that the 21st century consumer will only move and hit your link to purchase your product after you have entertained him enough. They will only give you their $25 when they finally get tired of seeing you after 25 people have testified on your behalf.

The 21st Century Entrepreneur must understand that even though Facebook has 2.23 billion active users, Instagram has 1 billion active users, and Snapchat has 191 million active users, which means what?

It means that all these social sites are oceans with different fish in them. Since you are a fisherman looking for fish to capture, you have to find out where the fish you are interested in are and look for them where they are already. I remember going to Israel in 2013 and the tour guide telling us that the number one fish in the sea of Galilee was the tilapia. And I remember that statement so much because it reminds me of the importance of location. You can't pray long enough for oranges to grow in Alaska the same way they grow in Florida. Almost a waste of time because the atmosphere is not conducive for that fruit to grow in that place. And the 21st Century Entrepreneur must understand this.

The 21st Century Entrepreneur understands that when you send a direct message to a prospect and the prospect completely ignores you, and you know that this person saw your message but didn't reply, not replying didn't mean that the prospect won't ever buy from you. It just meant 'not now, because they haven't seen enough to convince them enough to buy.' Or, 'I'm just going to keep consuming your free content until I can consume no more.'

The 21st Century Entrepreneur also understands that now this person has just started to notice you in the midst of this oversaturated world. The 21st Century Entrepreneur is aware of the fact that the 21st century consumer didn't buy because the consumer has billions of options. And because the Entrepreneur knows this, he must be willing to introduce himself to the customer because of the oversaturation that the marketplace has.

There is this amazing guy that I follow online that has made tears fall out of my eyes from watching him. However, I have only spent $100 with his business in the last 6 years, and I know that this person is amazing. But, in my opinion, this guy just doesn't ask enough, and that's the problem -- he is not asking.

The 21st Century Entrepreneur understands that he must ask and then ask 500 more times because you weren't listening the first 495 times because your eyes were watching, but your mind was busy. Or, your mind was already made up not to buy from the beginning. Because of that, the 21st Century Entrepreneur knows that the more you continue to follow their mission, that the more they build their case correctly to where they now ask for the 500th time, and ask you to buy, then you buy.

The 21st Century Entrepreneur is over-committed to the sport of business. He is committed to treating practice as the real game because they know that the way they approach practice is the same way they approach the real game. The 21st Century Entrepreneur is committed to the game of business because they know it is a game and he or she who is committed to the end is the person who wins.

The 21st Century Entrepreneur knows with all their hearts that the 21st century consumer is extremely judgmental. And because they know that, they make sure they can promote and advertise to their audience at every moment. They are not going to approach the moment in mediocrity because they don't need to give the consumer more to judge them on because they are already being judged, and they don't need to assist the consumer in what to judge.

The 21st Century Entrepreneur understands that if a customer didn't write a review or create a video to brag on your behalf in today's time, that means it never happened. The Entrepreneur needs to understand that testimonies matter in today's time, testimonies will save you millions and make you millions.

The 21st Century Entrepreneur must be an active learner in today's marketplace. It's essential to always study what other entrepreneurs are doing to see what's working and what's not working, to always be speaking the language of the day.

For example, recently I have applied to my selling strategies to always give beyond what the product actually cost. So if they buy something worth $5,000, I will give them something for free that's documented on my site that costs $1,000. I would just give it away, why? Because I have learned that when the offer is so amazing, they will never say no.

The person was probably not interested in the $5,000 product, he or she was really interested in the $1,000, but since it came for free, they wanted it and they refuse to pass it up. Lately, T-Mobile has been promoting that when you get a phone with them, you get Netflix for free. Same strategy, they are giving away so many bonuses that the bonuses become more important than the $375 you will spend to get started.

The 21st Century Entrepreneur must understand the 21st Century consumer is extremely educated about what they are interested in and because they are educated you must be even more educated because if your are not it makes the consumer not have trust in you to purchase from you.

The 21st Century Consumer is attracted to the person that can answer their questions, and because of that the 21st Century Entrepreneur must be a Master, a Wizard, a Magician someone who the consumer knows will solve their problems with their products.

With all this being said, if you want to prosper and do business in this economy, you must acquire some skills in order to do it in knowledge to attain what you want.

Let's get ready to acquire so that you can become!

List 3 things to become a better 21st Century Entrepreneur?

1. _____
   _____
   _____
   _____

2. _____
   _____
   _____
   _____

3. _____
   _____
   _____
   _____

CHAPTER 2

BECOME A MARKETER

Marketer: A person or company that advertises or promotes something.

A few years ago, a guy by the name of Mike Jones who was a local hip-hop artist from Houston officially shocked the hip-hop industry. Many people considered this guy's music to be extremely elementary and below average. They just laughed at him and completely underestimated this guy. I must admit I was a fan from day one.

But this guy did something that has never been done in history. The first thing he did was to give out his cell phone number on his music. The second thing he did was create a marketing campaign that was called, 'Who is Mike Jones?'

Those two things created a crazy buzz for him locally in Houston. Now please notice that I have not yet complemented his music. I didn't discover him because of his music, I discovered him because of his brilliant marketing skills.

Even though after giving out his cell phone number, it caught too much fire and he eventually had to change it and now the number was no longer good, it created massive attention. Plus, The Who is Mike Jones campaign was new at that time; no one else has ever done it. But many have attempted since, but that poster was everywhere. It was an absolute game changer. A major reason Mike Jones blew was because he was a great marketing genius.

In today's cluttered, crowded, saturated marketplace, you must know how to promote your business, yourself. Why? Because, if you don't know how, we won't ever know who you are. It is your complete responsibility that we know who you are. I tell people all the time that consumers are not thinking about you; they are barely thinking about themselves. You have to know how to promote your business.

SOCIAL MEDIA

Social Media has truly been the greatest thing to hit this country. Social media has made the world smaller and noisier simultaneously. But from the positive side, we have access to the world with a click of a button. We can see you on Instagram, Snapchat, YouTube, and Facebook on an everyday basis.

Years ago, when McDonald's had a new sandwich or chicken fingers they wanted to bring to our attention, they created a commercial and spent thousands on television ads. But now they can spend a portion of that because social media is where their world is at.

The whole world doesn't watch television like that anymore. Social media has truly made it a bit easier to market your brand. Facebook has 2.3 billion active users, Instagram has 1 billion plus active users. That's your ocean to swim into to market yourself every day.

DON'T DISAPPEAR, STAY VISIBLE

In 2016, I created a video called Interruption. And many people on Facebook really enjoyed the video in a big way. So, one day, I woke up to an inbox from a lady I have never met before.

Hey, brother, I sent you a coaching seed a minute ago. I need some help on this new level I'm entering really soon... thanks so much... blessings! That was her actual inbox.

The coaching session at that time, I believe, was $125 for a one-hour session. She ended up buying 2 more. She later bought a few other products from me. But what I want you to understand is that I have hundreds of videos, but it wasn't until she saw that video that made her spend money with me.

I look at my videos like music; you never know what record will bring you the recognition you've been looking for. I heard that some artists create 100 songs just to pick 15 for an album. The video caught her attention, but what if I had stopped creating, I would've lost that potential sale. I didn't disappear. She had probably seen me before but never stopped and paid attention because I didn't have the product that caught her.

McDonald's markets their products to you every single day. Why? Because they refuse to allow you to forget they are still there. Most of the times people don't stop there because we already know what's there, but when we discover that they have something new we are interested all over again.

COMMIT TO MARKETING

Imagine if you found somebody with a creative product that people would spend money for today, but the owner was extra introverted. However, you are a master marketer, and you have a strategy that you know can create income. Question.... Who is more valuable? The product or the marketer. I would say the marketer because you can take those same skills and promote another business, versus him with the incredible product; if no one knows of him, it would most likely stay in his living room.

Trust me I'm not saying he won't ever make it, but I'm saying that marketing is vital. You have to know how to make yourself known. We can't spend money if we don't know you exist.

Committed: Feeling dedication and loyalty to a cause, activity, or job; wholeheartedly dedicated.

You must be fully committed to marketing; I believe this is a non-negotiable thing. See, when you don't have marketing skills, you are basically waiting for someone else to acknowledge your greatness and for them to give you a hand and market your product. There is nothing wrong with that, but my point is, why wait and lose time? How much time will you lose in the process while you are waiting for validation?

Marketing is a major component to your success. They have hundreds of retired hip-hop and R&B artist complaining that the record label they were signed to didn't promote them right, so that's why the album was a complete flop. Instead of them complaining and taking responsibility and figuring it out themselves because it's also their own music and passion, they should learn to market themselves by themselves.

I remember seeing Jayz say that he wished that all the other artists in Rocafella had done what Kanye West did; he would have been happier.

Basically, Kayne became a master marketer. All the rest of the other guys disappeared when Rocafella split. All of them except Kayne. Why? Because he became more than just an artist, he became a marketer. Now please understand this, they all had skills to rap and create music as an artist, but they lacked one component which was critical to their success.

LEARN TO MARKET!

I promise you, I'm not a college graduate on marketing and branding, but one thing I did was to make a decision never to disappear. I believe the greatest thing I did was discovering who is already at the highest level in my industry and just duplicated that person in my own way with my own twist. I heard a coach one day say that the distribution company behind his book told him that for them to promote his next book, he must go live on Facebook 5 days a week to create a constant reminder to his audience that his book is out. And that strategy has worked for their former clients.

So, basically, the company is saying if you want to sell more books, you have to continue to market yourself in order for us to get behind your project. I promise you, the day I heard that, I knew exactly what I had to do to sell my first book. Before my first book, Principle, Participation, Promise came out, while it was still being edited, I was selling pre-order copies. I heard that marketing strategy and quickly applied it.

I'll tell you something, this very day, as I'm writing this book, a good friend of mine is doing a big party, and she has been going live on Facebook every day for almost two weeks straight. And today, I watched her live, and when she saw I was watching her video, she called out my name and pitched me to buy tickets for her event. I had to say yes, but imagine how many other tickets she has sold with that same simple yet effective strategy? But also think about how much money she is missing out on if she wasn't consistently marketing her event?

I hope I have convinced you about this marketing thing, because it is everything to your success in the marketplace. Please do yourself a huge favor and stop celebrating yourself privately and get out here and make yourself known in this noisy world. Go and command attention to your brand.

List 3 things to become a better marketer?

1. _____
   _____
   _____
   _____

2. _____
   _____
   _____
   _____

3. _____
   _____
   _____
   _____

CHAPTER 3

BECOME A SALESPERSON

Listen to me carefully, whether you believe it or not, everybody in business is a salesperson. I must admit that the word salesperson, for some ignorant reason, has received a bad reputation. However, whether you want to accept it or not, we are all salespeople. If you are a graphic designer, caterer, barber, personal trainer, realtor, MUA, etc., you have a product that you must sell in order for you to stay in business.

Back to the hip-hop artist in today's time -- 99% of them only see themselves as rappers that spend all of their days inside of a studio creating songs. So, that's why many of them never grow beyond the studio. None of them realize that once they stop rapping, they must become salespeople to attempt to convince us to buy their unknown music.

Listen to me, most rappers have no hustle, only a half-developed skill. Let's look at the website developer, even though he might be amazing, can he sell his service to the world? Can he fully and effectively explain to us why we need his service and how it can help our business? Only a salesperson can do that and do it correctly.

One of the greatest television shows to ever be on TV is Shark Tank. One of my favorite parts on the show is after the people finish pitching their product and bragging how it's going to change the world, the sharks ask the magic question. How are your sales? I have seen products that had all the momentum in the world completely drop in value in seconds because the sales were low or below the expected level. Why do the sharks get completely turned off? Because they don't want to invest in someone who can't sell.

Sales is the blood in the body. Selling is gas inside the car. Selling is why Amazon is putting people out of business, Netflix sells subscriptions, Spotify sells memberships, Coca-Cola sells soda, orange juice, coconut water, smart water, etc. The day my life changed is when I learned that I'm not just an entrepreneur, but a salesperson that is an entrepreneur.

Years ago, it never dawned on me that I was a salesperson. Most personal trainers know how to look all fit, but they have no idea how to sell their services. Most of them only know how to play defense in business, not offense. All they know how to do is react when the customer walks in; they have no idea how to pursue the customer, convert customers, and educate the customer.

The only reason you are not excited about your business today is because you are not selling enough. I promise you if you learn to sell every day, it will become amazing to you because then and only then will you learn that your income is determined by how well you learn how to sell.

3 Reasons why you must become a salesperson.

1. Explain your product

Here you are, the natural hairstylist, explaining to the walk-in customer who has a relaxer but is dying to be natural because she knows that the relaxer is truly frying her hair and that her hair is not being properly cared for. Believe it or not, this is selling. You are attempting to educate her on the benefits of why she must convert to going natural.

This is selling all day long, but see, when you don't know this is selling, you approach this moment of opportunity half way, not fully engaged with your potential client. And not knowing this can be the difference between you adding an extra $5,000 to your business because of her coming in on a monthly basis and a few of her friends and family coming to you because of her. This is something to consider.

I have a t-shirt that I have sold over 700 plus shirts, probably 1,000 by the time you read this. It says #self-employed in my mind; this shirt should be a self-explanatory shirt, but it's not, people ask me all the time, "What's the meaning behind the shirt?"

So, after hearing that question time after time, I had to create a sales pitch for it because I was losing sales because I couldn't explain my product. My sales pitch was basically, "I believe every human on this earth has some idea on the inside of them that is screaming to get out, and I'm just here to remind them of the idea." Boom, that was my line; that one line has brought me hundreds of dollars, all because I was able to explain my product. If you are a vegan chef, you must learn to explain why we must go vegan, why? Because going vegan is 1 billion times healthier.

The day I realized that my income was dependent on me selling, I took selling extremely serious. I have a great friend of mine by the name Tim Clark who is an app developer. This guy charges $6,000 to create an app for your own business. But guess what, he has to sell that service... I must admit I was so impressed with this guy to create a 6k product, but not just that, he is actually selling it, and people are giving it to him. That's incredible to me.

Now notice this, he is not just an app geek, he is also a salesperson. What's even more impressive to me is that I know Tim was first just an app geek. He had to learn how to sell his product. So, if he did not BECOME, he would not have created any income.

2.   Why you need my product!

I have a lesson that I call the Jehovah's Witness Principle. This principle is a true revelation to me because a Jehovah's Witness walks the streets, knocks on your door, and asks you for your time to sit down with you and explain to you why you need their religion. That's radical and necessary for you to have this skill in my opinion in today's marketplace. Their whole focus is to convert you to their religion and seeing the Bible the way they see the Bible, that's a sales job.

Here you are the, Vegan Specialist talking with your potential client that has diabetes and explaining why they must go vegan today and stop gambling with their lives. You must be willing to look them in their eyes with full certainty, full conviction, and say, "Ma'am, I completely understand that you love fried chicken, and you grew up your whole life eating this way, but if you don't stop, you won't make it to see 55, and you are 53 right now." You must be extremely serious about converting them to your product.

Convert: Cause to change in form, character, or function.

A person who has been persuaded to change their religious faith or other beliefs.

As a salesperson, you must be ready to convert people who are not on your product. You must understand that it's completely ethical for you to look at this lady dying of her sickness and sell her your services because you are a solution to her. See, as a professional salesperson, you actually do her a disservice not to convert her. Now if she claims she can't afford you, that's not in your control. But as a person selling a solution, not a product, you must convert her.

This Jehovah's Witness Principle gave me so much passion as a salesperson to have conviction, to attempt every day to convert people to me as an Entrepreneur Coach. My business relies on customers just like every other business in the world, so I must be converting new people to my products and services every day.

People tell me every day, "I don't want that audio program you are selling," and I say to them in reply, "trust me you might not want it, but you most definitely need it." Every time I say such a radical statement, they look at me in complete shock. That gets their attention every time, why? Because they meet someone aggressive and passionate about their business in this humble and passive world.

Let me tell a story about a company that I cold called here in Houston. I called this guy with the intent to set up an appointment with him. And when he heard my sales pitch, he told me I'm going to tell you right now I'm not interested at all, but if you are willing to drive up here, which was a 45-minute drive, I will give you 5 minutes to at least listen to you. (Please notice my drive was 45 minutes and he is only willing to give me 5 minutes). I said, "Ok, cool."

Now, where I'm from, when someone tells you they are not interested, that's exactly what they mean. But me knowing I have developed some skills in selling, I was willing to take the drive. My demo presentation probably lasted 6 minutes; he looked at me and said, "Let's do it."

I came back a week later and spoke for 30 minutes, and he handed me a check for $225. Remember, he originally told me he was not interested. But I know how to explain my product and explain why you need my product with full conviction in order to convert. I converted his original thought which was - he is not interested, to I'm completely interested, so interested that I will write you a check.

Now I know I have a premium product that the world needs, but I still have to sell it to them. Remember, I called him, I drove to him 45 minutes away, I presented to him, and I asked him for his business, I sold him.

3. You can't help them until they buy from you.

When I adopted this thinking to my arsenal in selling my products, all it did was set me even more on fire; I had no idea that I had more room for fire, but I did. Let's look at the personal trainer that's having a conversation with the overweight person who brought himself or herself to the gym because they were interested in being a healthier person for their own good. Most trainers love their career with their heart and soul, and they are very excited about the possibilities of seeing people transform their lives with their services.

But guess what? You can't partner with them until they first give you their debit/credit card and purchase your services. You can't start anything until they first buy, unless you work for free, which I sure hope you don't. Well, this really made more sense to me when I thought of MD Anderson, which is the number one hospital in the world for cancer patients. I have met people from all over the world here in Houston that have come to seek healing from this disease. But guess what, MD Anderson doesn't provide treatment for free; they sell treatment. Crazy, right? But it's called business, right? So, basically, they must sell you the service before they can help you. My audio teachings have helped hundreds of people, but they all purchased it before they heard it.

As an entrepreneur knowing this, I sell with extreme conviction because I want to truly help people learn how to prosper in their businesses, but I also know I can't help until they buy from me. You sell life insurance, right? Can you just go and give a non-customer a policy once their husband dies who didn't buy the life insurance package you offered while they were still alive? Absolutely not! Why? Because they didn't buy. Hard truth, but the complete truth.

2 THINGS YOU NEED TO BECOME A GREAT SALESPERSON

1. Education

You must be fully educated in what you do. The more you know, the more you can correctly educate us on what you do and why we need it. I spoke at Allstate recently, and one thing that I remember really drilling into them was, you must educate us why we need home, car, and boat insurance.

This might sound very elementary in this 21st Century, but the more you are educated, the more credibility you have with the client. The more you are educated, the more we trust that you can truly solve our problem. We buy from you to solve our problem. Blacks and whites go to the Spanish to get their cars fixed because the Spanish are the most educated in that industry. You must have knowledge of your industry so we can buy from you. Think about this, when you are fully educated in what you do, people will personally promote you because you helped them and their friends. That's what you want.

Educate: Give intellectual, moral, and social instruction to (someone, especially a child), typically at a school or university.

You must be able to explain intellectually to me why it would help me to buy from you versus the loss in not buying from you.

2. Sell with conviction

Conviction : A firmly held belief or opinion.

This is a word that you must never lose sight of, not ever. To sell in this economy or any economy ever, you must learn to sell and demonstrate your conviction. Conviction is defined as a firmly held belief. Steve Jobs launched and had success with Apple because he had conviction and was able to transfer that belief into his staff.

Donald Trump, with all the different approaches he took to defend himself before he became President, he had a belief; he had the conviction that he was the best man for the job. He was willing to call people out and say why they weren't the best person for the job. It was crazy watching all that and then to see him win. But, it was also very educational at the same time.

Remember the story I shared about the guy who wasn't interested, but then he purchased, that guy wrote a check to a guy that was convicted in his product. Hear me carefully my dear reader, the world is filled and infested with mediocre people, so when someone rises up with conviction, they instantly create attention and admiration today because 99% of the world is average.

Now, notice that I shared to be educated first because you can't sell without being educated first. Then you sell with conviction because your education enhances your conviction.

List 3 things to become a better salesperson?

1. _____
   _____
   _____
   _____

2. _____
   _____
   _____
   _____

3. _____
   _____
   _____
   _____

CHAPTER 4

BECOME A TECHNICIAN

This chapter is really tricky, and it's essential that it's understood correctly. A few years ago, I learned something while reading one of the greatest books in history ever written by Michael Gerber. In his book called the E-Myth, he shares how almost every Entrepreneur is a technician thinking he is an Entrepreneur. But, at the core he is really a technician. That book was extremely helpful to me to understand where I was and why I was struggling so much in business. Let's look at the definition of technician.

TECHNICIAN

A person employed to look after technical equipment or do practical work in a laboratory.

- An expert in the practical application of a science.
- A person skilled in the technique of an art or craft.

Let's take a very close look at the last definition. A technician is basically the hairstylist who is extremely talented at hair, but just in hair alone. So here she is sitting at her job crying every day at her job because she knows she is skilled in a technique of art.

But unfortunately for her, that is all she is skilled in without completely knowing that at all. So she quits her job to then discover that in order to be successful in today's economy she must master a few more skills like marketing, selling, etc. But she assumes that all she needs is to be more skilled in her art, but to then find out she only understood half the battle.

Now, I will explain my personal story of how not being a technician almost caused me to really lose my mind and completely doubt my dream one hundred percent. The day I committed my life to Christ, I knew God would put me in front of the camera, and I would have my own television show.

I was on television before I became a Christian, so it was just common sense to me. The only problem with this was, in 2008. I didn't get my own production going until 2013, five years later... why? Because I wasn't skilled in the art of editing my own videos of which now I have over 700.

This is what happened. In 2013, I went to Israel for 13 days. Before I went, I bought a camera in New York before I got on the plane. I got back from Israel and I was very excited about filming my show. But, to only still fall flat. Why??? I still didn't know how to edit, I was only skilled in being in front of the camera, but that wasn't what I needed; I needed production.

Luckily for me, or so I thought, I found two guys who were skilled in the art of filming. I was extremely excited to meet them and paid them their fee to see my vision finally come to pass that I had been believing God for since 2008. But these guys took the footage that I recorded and then gave me the finished work, and I handed them my hard earn money for an extremely average product.

At this point, I was upset and discouraged all at the same time. Then I met another guy who agreed to edit for me, and then one day I guess I caught him on a bad day and this guy officially cussed me out about how he does business. I was in complete unbelief in how he talked to me.

That night, I got home, and I sat at my computer and really prayed to God to help me figure this out. Then I finally decided to invest hours on YouTube (Thank God for YouTube) to finally invest the time to become skilled in this art of editing my own videos. By the grace of God and many hours of practice, I have now developed the skill to produce all of these videos.

Now, let me explain something very important to you so that you completely understand my viewpoint on this. I was not a technician at heart, or naturally, I had to become one.

Am I a 100% extremely gifted technician/video editor? Absolutely not, zero. But my vision to launch Thou Shall Prosper TV, commanded that I learn and acquire this skill in order to see my dream come to pass. Out of all the videos I have, only two videos were produced by someone else. And I could have done the job they did, even though I paid them as well because I was trying to delegate that to them. I knew and still know that being a technician is not my strong point. I had to attain this skill and attempt to bring this skill to the best level that would allow me to produce a video program that would be watchable.

I did not possess naturally the skills that I write about in this. I had to learn and to become them all. That's crazy, right?? But that's God's honest truth. If I could say I was anything, I would probably say I was a salesperson. I say that because I could speak well. But, I wasn't a skilled salesperson, which I am still becoming. But hear me and hear me carefully, I still hate being a technician till this day. I had to become one in order to see my vision come to pass. Why in the world do I keep repeating this? Because my vision required that I become a technician also.

Right now, at this very second, upon writing this book, my material is still not on iTunes and Spotify, and I see so many speakers with their material on these platforms, and I'm still clueless about how to do these things. But see, that's me not knowing the technical side of the business.

The problem for me is, I know how to create it in order to sell it, I know how to promote it, and also communicate it in order to sell. But my lack of the technical skill in making sure my content gets on these sites is hindering me big time. It's frustrating to me, but my desire in this book is to show you my great, my good, and my ugly.

THE PROS AND CONS OF BEING A TECHNICIAN

1. Pros

The benefit of being a technician in your process of developing your business is that in the beginning you really can't afford to pay someone to do the work. In my case, I had the money, but didn't have the money, but I was willing to find it.

In my case, becoming a technician helped me because it put me in a position to be self-sufficient. For example, if today I had a full-time video person, and then years later they decided to move on, I won't be stranded because they left. The show would still be able to move on.

I know many people who have dreams of launching all kinds of different projects but don't because they refuse to accept the role of the technician. And for me to watch from a distance, I know what skills they lack because I once walked in those shoes. You have no idea how amazing it makes me feel to see a video in my head and have the means to produce it the very same day or whenever I felt like it. It's extremely liberating.

2. The Cons

The bad side of being a technician is that you can't be everything. You heard the saying, too many people are the jack of all trades and masters of none. Being a technician or other things is completely not for everybody, that's obvious, right? So in the process of trying to become a technician, you might have to ignore what your dominant skill might be.

For example, I know I would have finished my first book a long time ago if I hadn't produced so many weekly videos. However, I was being so many things at once and I lost so much time trying to be a jack of all trades. So that's the downside, you lose time. Steve Jobs wasn't a technician, Steve Wozniak was. Steve Jobs didn't make computers, his partners did. Now, please, if you have a partner that's a technician, be grateful and let that person operate in their skill.

So there you have it, the pros and cons of becoming a technician. I know for me to see what I'm seeing today, I had to become a technician. I look at it from this point of view. I have a principle that I live by:

WITH GOD, I WALK BY FAITH, WITH MAN, I WALK BY SIGHT.

Now, even though I live by this principle, I also know that people judge me by this principle as well. I have intentionally shared an idea with someone and waited for their reaction without me demonstrating anything, and their reaction was absolutely flat. Then seconds later when I showed them the finished product of something, they have a million ideas for me because they saw something tangible.

But I know it's only the result of me accepting the role of the technician that has allowed me to manifest ideas; because I know how to create them and because I have acquired the skill of the technician.

List 3 things to become a better technican?

1. _____
_____
_____
_____

2. _____
_____
_____
_____

3. _____
   _____
   _____
   _____

CHAPTER 5

BECOME A SPEAKER

My last job before hurricane Katrina was in a restaurant as a waiter. I truly believe I was pretty good at my job. That job prepared me for my future and it taught me a few things. Number one, it taught me to make sure I was dressed as clean as possible because presentation is everything. Number two, it taught me how to adapt to multiple personalities that I encountered every single day.

Then years later, here I am in Houston as a hip-hop artist, and I was privileged to have had the opportunity to get on the radio. Then I started hosting a TV show called Hot TV which extremely helped me with what I'm doing today with Thou Shall Prosper TV. Then, because my reputation from the television granted me opportunities, someone asked me to host a concert with a very well-known local artist in Houston.

In my mind, I was thinking no big deal, that's the same skill I use to operate in front of the camera. I received the shock of my life. I remember looking into the crowd, and for a few seconds, I was speechless. See, on television, all you see is the camera. You don't have to look at faces, you can imagine faces, but you also know that no one sees it until it airs or it's posted online.

Well, I didn't know what I know now. To be a speaker, you have to have another skill, which is to be an entertainer. I remember looking at the people and for a second I felt like a complete failure. It was my first time hosting, and for my first time, there were hundreds of people in this club. Because the club was paying me, I wanted to be worthy of my hire. That day forever taught me that to speak in front of an audience, you must possess very important skills to be effective and engage the people listening to you.

You're probably reading this and thinking, "What in the world does being a speaker have to do with entrepreneurship?" I promise you it has everything to do with it. When you are an entrepreneur, you will forever be put in a position to have to speak to people and in front of people.

What I want you to understand is that when you suddenly run into someone at the mall and this person is interested in your business, you only have 30 seconds to effectively and passionately explain who you are. Similar to selling, right? But just a bit different. Most speakers are not salespeople, but all salespeople know they are speakers.

Let me explain. When Steve Jobs spoke to his company after they created the iPod, iPad, and iPhone, he stood in front of an audience introducing this new device with the intent to sell it to the whole world. But the speaker who is not a salesperson gets in front of the audience telling them about his product without passion and never explains to them why they need it, how much it cost, why he is so in love with it, who purchased it before them, how it's changing their life, and on and on.

That's why I committed my time to write this book to help you understand the extreme importance of all these skills so that you can become a monster in this marketplace.

A few days ago, I was on the phone with a client who bought multiple products from me. But while I was on the phone, I was selling my speaking package to this person also. See, this person didn't know I conduct business seminars. He thought I only did online videos. So, I discovered a major opportunity to reintroduce myself to him as a brand new person.

Have you ever heard of a guy named Warren Buffet? He is nobody important, just a guy that is worth 83.5 billion dollars. Well, this guy said that the greatest thing he ever did in his career was to invest in a public speaking course. When I heard that, I was completely shocked.

Here I am with that being one of my most dominant skills and a super billionaire is saying that was the best decision he ever made in his life. He said that skill helped him tremendously. What I have discovered is every person is an audience. Every interview is the interview before the next interview. And if you don't learn how to fully pull out your gift to speak correctly, speak for yourself, you will incorrectly present yourself.

Let's say I run into Larry at the gas station, and Larry and I have been casually running into each other for the last few weeks, but this was the first time we both decide to actually have a real conversation. Here we are attempting to find out what we have in common. I ask Larry, "What do you do?" and Larry says, "Nothing much, I work on computers." But what Larry was supposed to say is, "My company just created the first app in the world that has allowed every person in the world to just look inside of the camera in the morning, and the computer will read their thoughts just by looking at it and give them counsel according to their problems." I just made that up.

But I'm trying to explain how, because Larry is not a great communicator, he incorrectly presents himself and never makes a client because he lacks the skill of being an effective speaker. Let's say I would not have been interested even if he had explained himself correctly, but I could have become an extreme word of mouth spokesperson for Larry. You just never know what kind of moments you can create when you present yourself in the right manner.

FOUR BENEFITS OF SPEAKING

1. Command Attention.

When I first created my #Self-Employed t-shirts, for some reason, I wasn't fully confident in going into public places like barbershops, hair salons, going door to door in office buildings. I would rather open my trunk and let the people come to me.

When I think about it, it was just me being passive and lazy, even though, thank God, the shirts sold the same whether I opened the trunk or went inside of businesses. But I didn't know back then that I feared going inside these places because I didn't know how to command attention. I had to learn how to command attention.

Then one day, I was in Beaumont Texas. I went inside of this barbershop and spoke with so much power the entire place froze, and every eye came to me. Plus, I sold a few shirts. I left there wondering what the difference was. What made people stop and actually pay attention to me? I had the skill to get people's attention on a video, but doing it live was tough. What I didn't know is how to transfer that same skill to a live setting.

With the same skill, but live, you must turn it up 50x. You have to understand the shop was loud, noisy, and had a conversation flowing before you got there and to just walk in as a complete stranger, you better be worthy of interrupting them of the fun and entertaining conversation they already were having before you got there. So, commanding attention requires a few things.

2. Speak With Power

You can only speak with power when you know who you are and the value you bring to any table that you sit at or are invited to. When you speak with power, you demonstrate your passion, you demonstrate why they should pay attention to you. Why? Because you commanded that attention. See, me going into a barbershop was no different from the 15-second elevator pitch, but the barbershop is just tougher because you have 20 people listening, judging you, not paying attention, looking at their phone, watching the game, and playing the game. So, in my mind, I know I only have a few seconds to speak as someone worth listening to.

I once presented a seminar to a barbershop owner who wasn't interested in buying, but another barbershop owner walked up and said, "Bro, I have no idea who you are and what you are over here talking about, but something about you is drawing me to come over here and listen to every word coming out of your mouth." I knew what drew him, it was the power in my voice, my anointing, and my fragrance in the way I present my gift.

3. Communicate Your Message With Clarity

Clarity to me means simplicity; making sure your message is 100% understood. One day, my wife and I went house shopping. The lady at the builder's office was sharp. We didn't do business, but I could see that her speaking ability was sharp. She had power in her voice; she made sure she had a real answer to our questions. I actually asked questions I knew the answer to just see how well she would clarify the answer to me. But please notice I didn't say we went to a seminar, we went to an office and sat at a table with this lady, and we were her audience, and she spoke well.

Remember Larry? Larry didn't speak with clarity; Larry had no power. Unfortunately, Larry is only a technician and because he is only a technician, he lost an opportunity with me, and Lord knows how many others.

4. Speak the Language of the Day

As a speaker, you must know what people are interested in, not just what you are interested in. Lately, I have discovered that people gravitate to me when I start talking about the world being noisy, loud, cluttered, competitive and infested with mediocrity. It draws people to me because that's something everybody from every industry is wrestling with and having a tough time standing out in the midst of the noise. It's the language of the day. If you had a political podcast right now, you would be talking about Trump, Korea, the economy, taxes, is Trump a racist, why some rich white people hate Trump, etc.

That's the language of the day; you have to be relevant and revelatory all in the same conversation.

These are the things you must completely understand to become a speaker and activate your speaking skills in order to fully cash in on your entrepreneurship journey in today's tough and oversaturated world. While your competitor wants to hide behind a social media post, get out there and get loud, get clear and activate your voice so that you can command attention in this noisy world. Remember, we are not thinking about you, it's your job; to remind us of who you are and then when you command our attention, just make sure you actually have something to say and are worth listening to.

List 3 things to become a better speaker?

1. _____
   _____
   _____
   _____

2. _____
   _____
   _____
   _____

3. _____
   _____
   _____
   _____

CHAPTER 6

BECOME A NETWORKER

Networker: A person who interacts or exchanges information with others working in a similar field, especially to further their career.

To be a 21 st Century Entrepreneur, this skill is extremely important on all different levels. We are living in a time that I believe most people are righteously selfish, and what I mean by that is, everyone is super focused on their own projects which is awesome but that same focus causes blindness.

What I mean by that is, when you are super focused on your own deals, you become blind to other people's greatness. That's why Thomas Edison didn't recognize Nikola Telsa's gift when it was right there in front of him. Networking is a behavior, but also a skill. The way I have been able to move forward in business is because I'm an intentional networker.

When I see someone's uniqueness, I quickly create conversation to attempt to identify how we can collaborate in business in some way. The average entrepreneur is always self-centered and always trying to sell their own products, and most of the time don't even consider supporting others, which is bad because sometimes the quickest way to create relationships is to spend money with someone else.

2 REASONS WHY YOU MUST NETWORK

1. Everything you want in life is connected to someone else

One thing I have been really focusing on lately is that every human being on this earth possesses a different gift and everyone brings a certain skill to the table. One thing I do very well is to ask questions.

I learned from Dr. Mike Murdock that until you ask a question, your knowledge is accidental. That wisdom has really motivated me to always be ready to ask questions when I meet someone that is very involved in their business. Let's look at the definition again.

NETWORKER

A person who interacts or exchanges information with others working in a similar field, especially to further their career.

One thing I have realized is that when you are heavily involved in your industry, sometimes you tend to notice that it seems like everyone is doing the same thing, which sometimes that can be true.

One of my business partner's name is Andrew Hatton who has a business called Chill Tees, and he prints all my t-shirts. I'm pretty sure that if I wanted to, I could figure out a way to print my own shirts. But I refused to be so selfish and do that because I wanted to be connected to other people. My other business partner who created my audio programs, designs my artwork for my flyers and designs my book is a guy by the name of Bkelly. In my opinion, these people are extremely important for the function of my operation.

People are everything in business; you have no business without people. I have learned that the money you spend in business is a seed you are sowing into a future relationship. You will be surprised how much more of an ear someone will give you when you are spending money with them. I know most people don't like it, but it's the way of the world.

Look at churches around the world; they have people in the parking lot, kids' church, sound people, camera people, teenagers' ministry, etc. An average pastor's dominant gift is speaking and leading their ministry; they're not skilled in video editing or communicating with three year olds, so they have to know how to reach out to others and discover what the skills of others around them are.

2. It accelerates you.

One person can do more for you than 100 people put together. There is a story in the Bible about how they had kings from all over the world that paid a set rate every year to hear the wisdom of King Solomon.

1 Kings 10:23-25: So King Solomon surpassed all the kings of the earth in riches and wisdom. Now all the earth sought the presence of Solomon to hear his wisdom, which God had put in his heart. Each

man brought his present: articles of silver and gold, garments, armor, spices, horses, and mules, at a set rate year by year.

These Scriptures share how all these other kings around the world came to pursue the wisdom of Solomon to receive knowledge from him so that they could learn to run their kingdom better as well. To me, that is brilliant. These guys were applying what the definition of networking says, which is, especially, to further their career.

Networking is you saying to yourself 'who has what I need and what must I do to get in touch with them to learn what I don't know today.' These guys were pursuing wisdom to further the careers. That's why intentionality is a very important skill to possess in this self-centered world.

A few weeks ago, I read an article online that stated that if you want more engagement on your social media site, you must be engaging others so that others may know you are there. So many times I can admit I never realize that people are following me online until they comment on my post.

Let's go back to my hip-hop background. When a new artist is trying to get known, one of the things record companies do is to try to get a well-known artist on the music to attempt to get the unknown artist some attention and some creditability. Hopefully, for the unknown artist, the song is hot, so the unknown artist can accelerate their careers to get quick exposure. Now a well-known current artist might charge you 5k-15k for just one rap verse, but the success that it can bring you sometimes is truly unlimited.

I was with a business partner of mine who was telling me that his CEO actually wrote a check to a speaker for 50k just to speak at his conference for 45 minutes. Crazy, right, but I promise that speaker will never forget that young man for taking that leap of faith.

The conference will sell out because of that headliner. But understand the guy who wrote the check is just trying to accelerate his career. In his case, I actually think this was great, because in our case in the entrepreneur space, you need those kinds of relationships in your back pocket. Now I'm pretty sure he could have invested that 50k in 50 other things, but I'm pretty sure those other things would not have accelerated his career rate like this relationship.

In my opinion, networking to accelerate is crucial because we are racing against time. Time is running out every day. I just finished writing my first book, and one month later I'm writing my second, because I know this book will be a great networking tool to accelerate me pass the average talking people in the business world.

But time is our enemy, because the truth of the matter is, it will eventually run out for us all. I want you to make a true commitment as of today to devote your life to intentional networking because I'm pretty sure you want to accelerate your career, right?

Let's look at one of the greatest networking ventures that, as of lately in 2018, has been a true benefit for both parties. They have this new sports drink that recently hit the market in 2011 called Body Armor. In 2014, it caught the attention of Koby Bryant.

When Koby heard of the brand and discovered that the owners of the company had some involvement with vitamin water, Koby decided he wanted in. Now Koby is a shareholder and owns 10% of the company. One day while driving, I saw a YouTube video where Koby was speaking on his involvement with the company and how the brand is going to make James Harden one of the faces of the brand.

Since then, I have purchased bottles ever since I saw the video. why? Because of Koby. If I had not seen Koby speaking on their behalf, that product would have just been another bottle in the freezer inside of gas stations. But my point is, this company is cashing in big time because of the networking (accelerating their careers) with these credible names. Those Networking with Koby have fast forwarded their career 10 years because of the Koby connection.

Please, if you want to fast forward your mission and career, go and find someone to network with; it's impossible to make it in this world trying to do it alone.

List 3 things to become a better networker?

1. _____
   _____
   _____
   _____

2. _____
   _____
   _____
   _____

3. _____
   _____
   _____
   _____

CHAPTER 7

BECOME A SELF-PROCLAIMER

At the beginning of 2015, I had this incredible idea to call myself a Media Mogul. I remember when this idea hit me, one of the first things I did was reach out to someone and share my exciting news with this person. When I told him, the first thing he did was to tell me how I was crazy and how I didn't earn the right to attach that name to myself.

I must admit I was crushed because before I called him, I was so certain in my decision. I promise you, to this day, I still regret that I didn't stick to my conviction. I have not forgotten how I allowed this person's perception of me to kill my idea. Now, years later, I'm just discovering what it was that I was trying to do.

See, at that time, I was becoming what I am today, but because it was in my infant stage, I wasn't bold enough about my future, so I was easily talked out of it. This thing about being a self-proclaimer is so real to me; you have no idea how much this concept has transformed me. In this world today, we have a lot of people self-proclaiming who they are. I have learned that if I really want to dominate, I must be willing to do the same. If you're not careful, you will start thinking you are following the crowd by having the audacity to self-proclaim yourself.

Let me ask you a question. If you make the best chicken salad in the State of Texas, is it wrong for you to put that in your commercial, on your billboard, and outside on your window advertisement? I think not. I think it's more of a disservice for you not to. In today's crowded world, you must have the audacity to self-promote before we catch on to who you really are. Remember, we are not paying attention to you, it's your responsibility to remind us why we must pay attention.

Jesus Did It.

John 6:51: "I am the living bread which came down from heaven. If anyone eats of this bread, he will live forever;"

John 8:23: And He said to them, "You are from beneath; I AM from above. You are of this world; I am not of this world."

John 8:12: Then Jesus spoke to them again, saying, "I AM the light of the world. He who follows Me shall not walk in darkness, but have the light of life."

John 8:58 Jesus said to them, "Most assuredly, I say to you, before Abraham was, I AM."

John 10:9: "I AM the door. If anyone enters by Me, he will be saved, and will go in and out and find pasture."

John 10:11: "I AM the good shepherd. The good shepherd gives His life for the sheep."

John 10:36: "Do you say of Him whom the Father sanctified and sent into the world, 'You are blaspheming,' because I said, 'I am the Son of God'?"

John 11:25: Jesus said to her, "I AM the resurrection and the life. He who believes in Me, though he may die, he shall live."

John 14:6: Jesus said to him, "I AM the way, the truth, and the life. No one comes to the Father except through Me."

John 15:1: "I AM the true vine, and My Father is the vinedresser."

John 19:2: Therefore the chief priests of the Jews said to Pilate, "Do not write, 'The King of the Jews,' but, 'He said, "I am the King of the Jews."'"

When I read that Jesus was radical enough to self-proclaim himself, that he was willing to stake his claim to the people that were following him, you have no idea how liberating that was to me. The question is, was he lying? No. So, was he being arrogant? No. So what's the problem?

See, if you tell that to the wrong person, they will do to you what I allowed that person to do to me - talk me out of what I was committed to. All Jesus was doing was proclaiming who he was to those people so they could catch on.

This concept of being a self-promoter might be completely out of your comfort zone, which is understandable. It certainly was out of mine. Eventually, I had to embrace it because I saw that Jesus did it. According to most people, Jesus was the most humble person to have ever walked the earth. Jesus made, what we call in the business world, big claims. I am the good shepherd; I am the way, the truth, and the life; I am the true vine.

Back to you. What are you? Are you the best app developer? Are you the best life coach? Are you the best chef in your city? Do you have the best cleaning service in the State of Texas? If you do, I dare you to make the claim. I dare you.

DON'T WAIT TO BE VALIDATED.

If you carefully study success as I have, you will learn that the validation never happens. You must be willing to toot your own horn. Yes, I said it. The same people that try to humble you are the same people that are trying to be great and rich also. But they will try to dumb you down if you let them. Be very careful with that.

A few weeks ago, I was watching an interview with Elon Musk, and the interviewer asked him what gave him creditability to go into the space business? And Elon answered, "I have just read a lot of books and did a lot of research." And the interviewer in the most sarcastic way said, "So you are self-taught?" And Elon said, "Yes." Elon was crazy enough to believe and validate himself. If you are waiting to be discovered and for someone to give you a permission slip to be great, I promise you will be waiting forever, and it won't happen.

VALIDATION

Recognition or affirmation that a person or their feelings or opinions are valid or worthwhile.

When you sit around and wait to be affirmed by the opinions of people, you will be waiting the rest of your life. Then you wake up at 45 and realize that you lost 20 years of your life because you waited for someone to give you affirmation.

I promise you I know what I'm talking about because I have received permission from people, not verbally, but by motivation alone. After the fact, I realized that it wasn't until this person did that for me that I was stuck until they gave me a pass. You have no idea how heartbreaking that is, because I would be playing with this thought in my head for months and then here comes this person that affirmed this thought, and now all of a sudden I was excited to move forward. That's not right.

In 2015, I was invited to speak at a conference by a great friend of mine by the name Jarrod Wilkins. This event had multiple speakers with one headliner who didn't show up. I spoke at the event, and I promise you I crushed it.

I sold so much product after the event, it was amazing. The whole night I was just high on life. Then, when my wife and I got home, we began to talk about me doing my own events just like that but with only me as the speaker.

We came up with a plan to execute, and we committed to doing the events. Then after all the planning, I looked at her and said, "Wow, all these years it has been in my heart to do my own events, but I didn't believe in myself enough to do my own events. I never knew that people would be willing to come and hear me speak all this time. I have been waiting for a pass, and this event just gave me validation to finally believe in myself."

It absolutely freaked me out because my next thought was, "What if the validation never came?" I would be still stuck until this day waiting for someone to give me the opportunity.

YOU ARE JUST BEING HONEST.

Let's say you have the greatest bar-b-que in the state and then you decide to create your own bar-b-que sauce to sell because you are so confident that it's the best and you put on the label the best bar-b-que ever created. Are you lying or are you telling the truth?

Back to Jesus. Did he have proof that he was the way, the truth, and life the second he spoke it? He didn't, but did he say it anyway? He did. Why? Because he believed it and that was enough for him to be willing to make that claim. Powerful, right? I want you to be honest with yourself. Listen to me. No one, I mean no one, will ever believe in your greatness until you do. And we won't believe until you make us believe.

What I want you to understand is, if you are not willing to brag on yourself, all you are really doing is lying to yourself, about yourself. If you have the goods, make it public. I know this belief is not popular but it's a belief I had to adopt.

Most people wait their whole lives for someone to give them permission. Who in the world permitted me to write a book? God did, then I gave me permission. Most people wait for a human to give them permission to fulfill their purpose on this earth; that's crazy to me.

They sit in the church for 20 years, and then someone walks up to them and tells them God told me to tell you to start writing the book. Then they leave the church all excited to finally start doing something that God himself told them 500 years ago, just because another mortal being gave them permission.

I know I sound very adamant on being rebellious about not waiting for permission from people. But I promise, I was unconsciously a slave to that frame of mind but not knowing I was. I was silently waiting for permission, I just didn't know I was until I finally received validation. Be honest with yourself; you owe it to your future.

FALSE HUMILITY

We don't make a lot of decisions in life because of what I call false humility. There was a book written years ago called The 48 Laws Of Power. And one of the laws gives an analogy that if there is a room full of people and a question is asked and you know the answer but are fearful of raising your hand to give the answer, and someone else is willing to raise his or her hand and give the answer, that person deserves to be further in life than you because they had enough courage to stand in front of people and give the answer.

False humility will have you dumbing yourself down so that you can be accepted among the mediocre. False humility is the newspaper walking into your store and saying we heard on social media that this place has the greatest pork sandwich in the world and because of that we called Channel 8 to put you on the local news all day today. And you look at them and say, "No it's ok, I'm just a little farm girl that just knows how to season meat the best way because my grandmother taught me right." And you miss the opportunity to have free attention from the local news that would have exposed you to city and created more business for you. That advertising normally would cost you $15,000.

In my opinion, false humility is so deadly. It makes you accept a version of yourself that you are not. If you were created to be Michael Jordan, why die being Luc Lonley? No disrespect to Luc, but don't allow the spirit of mediocrity to rob you of your true potential.

Being willing to conduct my own events and make myself the headline speaker was in my heart, but I was struck with fear. It wasn't until I was willing to self-proclaim myself and make myself the headline speaker and the only speaker that I began to walk in my full potential and then the rest was history.

List 3 things to become a better self-proclaimer?

1. _____
   _____
   _____
   _____

2. _____
   _____
   _____
   _____

3. _____
   _____
   _____
   _____

CHAPTER 8

BECOME A MANAGER

This chapter is very scary to write, but it's extremely important that I write it because management is a skill you must possess to develop a business, but not a skill to grow a business.

MANAGEMENT IS ORGANIZATION.

Most people today have no idea that Ray Kroc didn't start McDonald's; they're two brothers in California who started McDonald's, but the brothers were managers.

They weren't entrepreneurs. They were managers, meaning they were skilled in organization. So, they basically were in love with the idea of making sure every hamburger had only two pickles on it. Ray Kroc was in love with the idea of planting a McDonald's in every city in the world. He even mortgaged his house to go into debt to see this vision come to pass.

But let me explain why management is important. In this life, you prosper based on what you can manage. The more you can handle, the more you qualify for. If you can't handle 50 people in your restaurant, why in the world will you go and get a bigger location that holds 200 people at one time?

Management is important because management creates order and order creates peace. Management allows you to know what's coming in and what's going out. The reason this book is written is to help every entrepreneur in the world understand that we need multiple skills to be successful, but to also educate us in what we lack and why it's urgent we fix it or find someone to put in place to solve that problem.

For example, the responsibility of the manager at McDonald's is not to grow the company. His responsibility is to keep it organized. His job is to make sure the restaurant is functioning at the right speed, to make sure the orders are getting out at the right speed, to make sure the employees are not stealing money and food, to make sure the employees are not giving an extreme amount of ketchup for no reason, etc. His job is to keep order.

As an entrepreneur, my job with my t-shirt business is to know how many t-shirts are in stock and to be able to predict the timing when I will be out of shirts and order them beforehand so I'm never caught without shirts. This is the same thing the manager at McDonald's is doing - ordering the burgers, buns, and fries ahead of time to keep the business organized.

Most entrepreneurs today are only focused on selling, speaking, and promoting, which is super important but they have never realized they lack management. You can have millions of dollars flowing through your business, but if you can't prove it to the bank, it doesn't mean anything. And that's why it's important to have your management skill in operation at all times.

Management allows you to plant the grape seed, tend to the grapevine to eventually create grape juice, wine, and grape jelly, and then put your entrepreneur hat on and then go and sell it to the grape lovers. But without the manager, that grape jelly would never come to exist.

Look at this Scripture from the book of all wisdom.

Proverbs 27:18: Whoever keeps the fig tree will eat its fruit;

This Scripture is saying what I just finished explaining about the grape seed. The grape seed must be cared for in order for it to become grape jelly. This scripture is saying that when you keep the tree you have planted in the ground, then the time will come that you will have the pleasure to eat and enjoy the fruits that are hanging on your tree.

But the problem with most entrepreneurs today is that we are not excited about managing, we are only excited about promoting, which generates a lot of attention, and selling, which creates income, but management is what allows that company to even have something to sell and promote. The grape jelly doesn't exist without someone watching that seed day in and day out to eventually become a real product to one day be able to sell.

I believe Management allows you to do two things:

1.   Maximize

When I first started selling CDs on the streets of Houston, I was paying $1 per CD and I was selling them for $5. Here I was paying

$100 to make $500. Knowing that each CD was worth $5 allowed me to place a high value on every last CD that I had in my possession.

When I think of the word maximize, I think of squeezing every ounce of possibility from what it might ever be. If I'm selling watermelon juice and each watermelon allows me to make 5 drinks from it, that means to me as the entrepreneur/manager, for lunch, I'm not drinking watermelon with my lunch, I'm drinking water. Because if I have 100 watermelons and I'm selling each watermelon drink for $3, once I have sold each drink, I will have $1500. As the manager, I'm committed to making every last cent I could from every last watermelon.

In the streets, they have a super important principle that says, "Don't get high from your supply," which basically means the same as not drinking your watermelon drinks. As a manager/entrepreneur, you must be extremely committed to maximizing every last resource that is available to you so you can then move to step two.

2. Maximize to Multiply

Here you are with $1500 from your watermelon juice profits. What do you do next? You reinvest to repeat the process.

It's simple math. You save $1000 and invest $500 and buy $500 worth of watermelons. Let's say you get watermelons for $2 each at wholesale. You have 250 watermelons that you can sell the juice from for $15 each watermelon. This means you now have $3,750 worth of watermelon juice sales. Now you have $3,750 worth of sales.

But I promise you, without disciplined management, none of this happens. Millions of entrepreneurs are great at selling, promoting, speaking, networking, and yet struggle to multiply their money even though they create it.

Management allows you to know what's coming in and what's going out. Imagine the feeling of seeing yourself make $750,000 last year, but not having a single dime to show for it. Management gives you the discipline to drive a Honda CR-V when you truly desire a Cadillac Escalade, but you are truly determined to exercise your management skillfully.

Never forget that we manage to multiply, not manage to maintain and never to expand the company. The story I told earlier about McDonald's is so important to understand. Please go and watch the movie called 'The Founder'. This is the whole McDonald's story about how the McDonald's brothers started McDonald's in California but didn't know how to expand the company. Even worse, they were content with managing the one store they had already.

They had absolutely no desire or vision for growth, zero. Here comes this salesman who was selling them milkshake machines. He came to their restaurant all the way from Missouri and was confused about why they wanted such a large order of milkshakes machines. But, he drove all the way to California and when he saw the first McDonald's store, he fell in love.

He finally got them to permit him to start franchising their creation, and within months, he had more stores than they had had in years. But the greatest problem they had was, they were managing just to keep order, not to expand. And that's the downside of managing. Most manage to just manage, not to expand.

That's why the chances of a restaurant manager starting his own restaurant and him being successful are very slim. Because his true skill is managing, not expanding. The average manager is inside of his place of business consumed with the thought of just running his operation and going home at the end of the night, not in growth.

With all this being said, make sure you are always obsessed with the thought of managing to multiply.

List 3 things to become a better manager?

1. _____
   _____
   _____
   _____

2. _____
   _____
   _____
   _____

3. _____
   _____
   _____
   _____

CHAPTER 9

BECOME A NEGOTIATOR

Negotiation is a master skill that very few people are interested in because negotiation means having tough conversations even when you don't feel like it. It is the ability of trying to enforce your way on people when they don't agree at all.

One important thing about negotiation that has made negotiation important in the business world is that you never get paid your worth; you get paid what you negotiate.

Negotiation is something I'm in love with. Most times I negotiate just for sport. The majority of the times I really don't need a deal. I'm just intentionally testing my skill to keep it sharp. Negotiation is something I believe is important for the buyer and the seller.

Let's start off with the seller. The seller's job is to get his asking price for his products and services regardless of the buyer's perception of what the seller is saying it's worth to him. Negotiation goes along well with being a salesperson and speaker. The salesperson in you allows you to articulate what you are selling effectively and the speaker in you allows you to speak with clarity what you are trying to get them to understand.

Let me share an example about negotiating from a seller's stance. I have multiple products that I sell as an entrepreneur, but let me simplify it by sharing an example from two different products. My CD product is $7, and it costs me 45 cents to create it. My shirts are $20, and it costs me $8 to create. So, here I'm talking to a walk up that I attempted to sell the CD.

Me: Good evening, my name is JJSimmons. This CD has 31 lessons I will be teaching on entrepreneurship, would you like to purchase a cd for $7?

Customer: No sir, I'm really broke.

Me: Would you like to purchase a shirt instead? (Remember, they just told me they're broke.)

Customer: How much are the shirts?

Me: $20

Customer: How much is the CD again?

Me: $7

What did the customer just reveal to me? That they are not broke. What I know as a salesperson is that the CD didn't have the perceived value to them because they truly have no idea what's on it and what they could potentially receive from buying it.

Customer: You know what, I can buy the shirt, I have some shoes to match.

Me: Thank you much.

Sometimes I might throw the CD in there as a bonus just to show appreciation; it depends on their body language towards the CD. But remember how this conversation started. They told me they were broke.

Where I'm from, broke means broke, but in reality, broke doesn't mean broke, it really means I'm on a tight budget and I'm trying my best to resist myself from purchasing because I've been spending all week.

Now, as a negotiator, why would I ask them to buy a $20 shirt after they told me they couldn't afford a $7 CD? Because as a negotiator I have been involved in so many sales predicaments that I have learned how to interpret words to know what the buyer really means. Negotiation skills are important in business because it will determine how you get compensated in the marketplace.

Now let's transition to me being the buyer.

BUYER

Proverbs 20:14: It is good for nothing cries the (buyer) But when he goes his way he boasts.

The Scripture is saying that the buyer looks at a product the seller is attempting to sell him, and he says it's good for nothing, meaning it's worthless, the asking price is insane, I will never buy this at this rate. That's what the buyer says to attempt to devalue the product and the price. But after he convinces the seller that it's worthless, and the seller gives in to the buyer, the buyer then leaves knowing he got an incredible deal.

Now, this is why negotiating from a buyer's perspective is extremely number one. It will allow you to save money for your business, and it will allow you to never settle for what you are not interested in.

I remember one day I was at an appliance store looking for a few things to buy because I just moved into this place and I had no furniture in it. Out of nowhere this guy walked up to me and began to tell me that he just got a call to report back to the military and must sell all of his furniture asap because he has to leave in two days. So I asked him if he had a kitchen table and he said yes.

Me: How much?

Customer: $150

Me: I will give $100

Customer: ok

So I followed him to his house to look at the table.

Me: This the table? (Me showing complete disinterest.)

Customer: Yep

Me: Nah bro, I can give you $75

Customer: Ok

I saved $75 because I was willing to ask for another price. In this case, I had data on him. He was in a rush to get back to the military which meant to me it was urgent that he got rid of everything he had. This allowed me to put him in a position to make a quick and emotional decision.

Many people don't know how to negotiate, so they are led to believe they have to take any deal that gets presented. In a negotiation, it's ok to say no and walk away from the table; it's completely ok.

I remember a good friend of mine telling me how a company was trying to sell him some shirts on a business deal and he was highly upset because[CG1] he said he had to pay his employees upfront from money he really didn't have. I looked at him and just told him it's ok to say no.

This guy was trying to be grateful for the business by sacrificing to do whatever he had to do to complete the job, which is important. But, at the same time, I'm pretty sure if he had estimated correctly what his price was for his service, he would have never been in that position. You will be surprised how much more the deal can go your way if you are just willing to ask for the price you really want.

Negotiating is the ability to allow the other person to see your point of view and agree with your side. Does it happen all the time? No, but you never know if you will get your way if you are not attempting to ask.

I negotiate everything, I never accept price number one, never. Because I always know there is hope to lower the price. Let's say someone is attempting to sell me something for $225 a month and we agree to $185 a month. I just saved $420 for that year. Let's say it was a security system that I will have for the next 50 years. I will save $21,000, which matters to me significantly. To me, this is me also having my manager hat on fully, maximizing my resources. But that savings will not have happened without me knowing how to negotiate.

Negotiation sometimes might create offense to the other person, but if you want your way in the business transaction, you must be willing to offend, of course not on purpose, but at the same time on purpose. I had a guy a few days ago who offered me $10 to buy my book; I looked at him like you are out of your mind. But guess what, that was his offer and I simply just said no.

I had another young lady the same day who told me she was broke at least three times. I kept going back and forth with her because when people tell me they're broke, I never believe them anyway. I said ok if $20 is too much, just give me $19.99, and guess what, she sent me $19.99 on the cashapp. Unbelievable, right? But it really happened.

List 3 things to become a better negotitator?

1. _____
_____
_____
_____

2. _____
   _____
   _____
   _____

3. _____
   _____
   _____
   _____

CHAPTER 10

BECOME A LEARNER

Learning has probably been the master key of my life. When I was young, I really had developed the mentality that whatever talents you have in life, those were what you are stuck with and really had no choice or decision making in the deal. In 2010, I ran across a Scripture in the Bible that really set me on fire; this one Scripture forever set me on a trail that truly helped me indeed. Without this key, Lord knows where I would be today as a person.

Proverbs 1:5: A wise man will hear and increase in learning.

This Proverb helped me to understand that whatever I wanted to learn, all I had to was hear it and continue to hear it as much as possible. You would think I knew that, but I truly didn't because I grew up hating school. I went to middle school and high school high every day for four years straight. Learning was the last thing on my mind. I basically went to waste time and get the school day out of the way.

So in 2008, when I gave my life to Christ, as an ex-rapper, I truly thought that from that point on my life had no true significance. I had the frame of thought that my life would be pretty much average. Then one day I was blessed by a friend who gave me an audio lesson. And in this lesson, I heard this Scripture in Proverbs 1:5. This master key gave me the permission to learn.

WHY YOU MUST LEARN

As an Entrepreneurship Coach, I have come to this revelation: I am not valuable in this economy unless I really have something to teach and share with people. This age is saturated with people who pull out their phones and believe they have something to share, which 99% of them don't. But the point is, most of them actually have an audience that entertains their content. As long as they have an audience, they have a platform that they can and should maximize, and some even monetize as long as the audience is there.

Everyone today has a message. That is crazy, but I must admit, I respect the hustle. Most of those people are not educational, but they are marketers. So, for us that are true students of this thing called entrepreneurship, we must stay fresh with true substance to our messages. You can only teach what you have; you can't bring people through your teachings where you have never been.

7 THINGS LEARNING HAS DONE FOR ME

1. I Learned to Develop My Personality

When I first started on my Entrepreneurship journey in 2005, I had zero skills in selling. I had zero entrepreneurship personality. I was just operating in my natural state of being me with no understanding that I had the potential to manufacture a greater version of myself. One day I came across a book by a guy named Frank Bettger called, How I raised myself from failure to success in selling. This book helped me tremendously.

This book was about a guy who was a baseball player in the major leagues and one day in training camp before the season even started, his coach cut him. This guy was crushed, he could not believe what his ears heard. The coach looked at him and said, "I fired you, not because you lack talent, you just have zero passion, you have no enthusiasm." The coach went on to say how he watched him the whole time at practice and he noticed that Frank portrayed that he had no interest in being there, so for that reason he was cut.

Frank was cut that day and was never allowed to play for another team ever. He left that job to go on to sell life insurance. When he entered that career, he never forgot his old coach's words. From that day on he made it a habit to practice enthusiasm. Correct -- practice enthusiasm. When I read this, I knew in my heart that I discovered a golden gem forever.

At this point in my entrepreneurship journey, I never knew that I could intentionally transform my personality with a simple decision to change it. I thought up until this point that whatever way I was feeling that morning was the way I had to function for the rest of the day. I thought that I had to wait for motivation to come over me whenever motivation was ready to find me. I truly didn't know that I had control in the situation. That story taught me that. But it came because of my passion for learning.

2. I Learned to Edit Videos

Editing videos were something that was hunting me like crazy because it was connected to the vision I had for my life. From 2006-2008, I was a part of a tv show called Hot TV, by my dear friend,

Malik Rasheed. Malik was so graceful to me that he allowed me to be a host on his show. I had no experience, but he gave me a shot. I actually turned out to be pretty good at it. But after that season of my life ended, I was stuck because I had a desire to start producing my own content. But my problem was that when I was working with Malik, I was just in front of the camera and never learned the behind the scenes.

So here I am in 2008, with a God-given vision to start my own show and an expensive camera. That camera is a dinosaur today. Having the camera didn't even matter because I couldn't produce anything because I didn't know how. Between 2013 and 2014, I began to pay different people to edit the film that I would bring them, and they still weren't giving me the value that I truly wanted to.

One day, one of them, for some reason I don't remember, cussed me out. I promise, I was so stunned. That day, I went home for at least four hours and prayed. I intentionally sat in front that desktop until I understood it. Today I'm so glad to say I have 800 plus videos online. I produce my TV show that gets aired in Houston, Texas that has more than 5 million people in this incredible city. But my vision was hindered back then because I lacked a skill that I now was able to acquire because I was willing to learn it.

That skill connected me to learning, not crying, begging, wishing, hoping, and kissing tail to live in my destiny. All I had to do was have the willingness to invest time to learn and develop this skill that I desperately needed. This was real as oxygen to me because my dreams were connected to this vision.

Film is a true passion of mine. When I really sit and think about how my dreams would have been on hold had I never sat in front of that computer that night heartbroken. But I knew that I needed to develop this skill. On the flip side of that, if I hadn't invested the time, I would still have been waiting for someone to see my struggle and decide to be on my team to help launch this vision.

I watched Mark Zuckerberg being interviewed one day, and he said something that really inspired me to keep going. He said, "They had other companies that had more money, workers, engineers, and servers than us, but we created Facebook because it just mattered more to us, so that's why they were able to succeed, because it mattered. That really lit a fire in me because I had no money, just a dream and strong desire to launch this God-given vision of mine. But it was connected to my passion for learning.

My destiny was connected to my willingness to learn.

3. I Learned to Sell My Products

When I first began to learn to sell my products with more professional skill, my life changed for the better because I began to understand that my income wasn't determined by the potential customer alone. I learned that I had a participating role in the transaction.

Before I began to get skilled in selling, I had what I heard Jarrod Glandt called personality success, which means I relied on personality alone. That means I didn't know how to transform my personality in a sales transaction, which meant that my income was limited because I was relying on my personality to help me in a sale, not my skill.

Let me give you one example of how I learned to sell that I believe saved my entrepreneurship journey: Me: Hey ma'am, would you be interested in buying this audio program. It has 31 lessons with me teaching business principles that would increase your income?

Lady: No, I'm broke.

Me: Would you be interested in buying a shirt?

Lady: How much are the shirts?

Me - $20

Lady: Oh I really like the shirts.

Me: What size do you wear? A medium? (I can look at anyone and know their size by just looking at them because of my experience in the t-shirt business.)

Lady: How much is the entrepreneurship lessons?

Me: $20

Lady: I don't have no money.

Me: I take cards, I have the square card reader.

Lady: Starts laughing really hard. She says ok let me go inside the store and get cash back and then I will buy.

Me: If you will buy then let's just do it now!

Lady: Ok

Why was I able to make this sell? Because my mentor Grant Cardone taught me to treat the buyer like a buyer and then the buyer will become a buyer.

Before, my sales approach was judgmental. I know it sounds horrible, but that was my thought process. I would only talk to people that I perceived to have money. That approach hindered me big time. I didn't know how to help the customer make a decision. I never knew there was such a thing until Grant Cardone helped me with that. I didn't know that you can learn to sell. But I do know there is a skill to this thing called sales, which I have learned, and I continue to learn every day. I watch segments of Grant Cardone every single day because I know I'm investing in my skill and future.

Remember Proverbs 1:5

A wise man will hear and increase learning.

Hearing Increases Learning.

4. I Learned To Pursue Mentorship

Pursue :Follow (someone or something) in order to catch or attack them.

The year 2010 was a very special year for me. If you read and listen to my material, you will always hear me reference the year 2010. That year, I heard John C. Maxwell say that when he was a young man, he had this idea to look through his rolodex and call every successful person he knew. He would ask them if he could invite them to lunch and ask them a list of questions so that he can improve his life for the better with the intent to create the possibility of them mentoring him.

When I heard him say that, it was a complete illumination moment for me because I knew it was a key to unlock heaven for me. I had problems that I didn't know the answers to, and I needed them answered fast.

I decided to do the same. I looked through my cell and invited every successful person I knew to lunch to ask a list of 21 questions that I created. It was probably the best thing I've ever done in my life. The greatest thing that it taught me was to just pursue the mentorship, and it would happen.

One thing I learned was that highly successful people are extremely willing to give counsel to people because most of the people they know only want their money, not their wisdom. For them to see a younger person in pursuit of their goals is amazing to them.

MY DR. MIKE MURDOCK'S STORY

Dr. Mike Murdock is a televangelist who is on Christian television every night. I just fell in love with his teachings because his words were just major in my life and where I was trying to go. I remember in 2010-2012, I would watch him on television every night. Listen, every night, and I promise it was the very same show on repeat. I watched it every night for two straight years.

In my heart, I knew that one day I would meet this amazing man that I just idolized. One day, I heard he was coming to Houston. By this time, it's 2015 and I had just started my own television program, Thou Shall Prosper TV. I showed up to his event, and I walked up to him and asked if I could interview him, and he told me that he would. When the event ended, he told me he didn't have time and he apologized. I promise, I was hurt, but I knew he would keep his word to me. About six months later, he came back to Houston, and this time we did the interview.

That interview really helped me tremendously in building my reputation in the media world, because every pastor knows Dr. Murdock. In 2017, he sent a call to all his followers via voice message where he announced that he was hosting a conference, Five Days of Glory, at his church in Fort Worth. I just knew in my heart I had to go. I drove to Fort Worth from my home in Houston, which is a 4-hour drive.

I got to the church and I discovered that the event was only inside of his media studio inside the church. They were only streaming to the public and I had to watch it from the sanctuary. Imagine me sitting inside this church knowing I just drove 4 hours just to be able to shake my mentor's hand and look in his face and just say thank you for maybe just 30 seconds and then drive back home at 10:00 at night to maybe make it home at 2-3 am. I was upset.

By the grace of God, one of his assistants was walking down the hallway and noticed me and remembered me from the interview, I was so happy. I asked him can he please get me inside the studio. He went back inside and came back to get me and boom there I was inside his media studio. When he finished, I walked up to him and just fell on my knees in tears in complete honor. I was so grateful to look in this man's eyes; you have no idea. He talked to me for maybe 25 minutes and told one of his staff members to bring me to the bookstore and give me all the free material that I wanted.

I went and got a few things. Then I was off and on my way home. The next morning, I was like in heaven because of what happened the day before. Then I decided to go back. I went back and forth to Fort Worth three days straight, which means I drove a total of 24 hours just to pursue and be in the presence of my mentor.

That's my point to you. Before 2010, I didn't know that I had to pursue the mentor. I thought that one day someone would recognize my hard work and be kind enough to offer to help me. I didn't know that I had to make myself known to them and chase them down because they have what I need, I don't have what they need.

Highly successful people meet all kinds of people from all walks of life. They have met people who claim to be serious about their goals but then when the mentor says stop doing this and do it like this, they resent the mentor. They have met people who appear to be interested in what's in their hearts, but the whole time were just interested in what's in their hand.

These people have met all kinds of personalities, so none of them are impressed with mere words because they have heard it all. But I promise you, they respect pursuit because they know that the hungry pursue, because they are truly passionate. If you would make the decision to pursue, to chase down the mentor until you get his or her attention, you would be amazed at what could happen for you.

MY GRANT CARDONE'S STORY

One day in 2016-17, while watching my daily Evan Carmichael YouTube motivation videos I ran across Grant Cardone. Something about this guy connected me to him. Maybe it was his radical side on display through the videos. I have no idea, but I saw something in him that I needed. It took me maybe a full two years to find out what it was that Grant did, which was sales and real estate, but I just kept watching because something was there.

In the summer of 2017, for some divine reason, I began to watch him every day for like a month straight. I was in New Orleans at the time, and one Sunday morning, I decided to visit Bishop Lester Love,

The City Of Love. And Bishop Love in the beginning of his sermon said that he was reading a book by a guy named Grant Cardone called Be Obsessed Or Be Average.

I couldn't believe what I was hearing, plus he had the picture of Grant on the projector. I was stunned for many reasons. One, because I was already watching every day around that time. Two, because I would have never imagined that Bishop would be reading Grant Cardone. I don't know why, but it was just a shocker. And three, like what are the odds of that happening? I was super late to service that day because I couldn't make my mind up about what church to go to that morning. I believe to this day that I went to see that. I felt certain that this was confirmation that I was in season to what God had me doing, which was learning from Grant.

Around the same time, Grant was doing a conference called The 10X Growth Con, which I didn't attend, but I paid to have access to the live stream that I decided to buy. One Sunday morning, I was watching him on Live Instagram, and he announced that to those who brought the live stream to one person, he would give a free coaching session to. Guess who won it? You guessed it, JJSimmons, yours truly. We did the coaching session.

Right now, this day, while I write this, that video, called Your Numbers Matter, has 37k plus views. A few months after we did the session, I saw his dear wife on Instagram page @elenacardone that they were on their way to Houston and I sent her a DM, and she replied and sent me the location. I showed up to the spot while they were walking out of the restaurant and I did a quick interview with Grant. That day, @johnnythecameraguy [FB2] was with him, and he was Grant's camera person and also films it on his camera.

To my surprise, Johnny put a video together that is called Who is Grant Cardone on YouTube that right now, as I'm writing this, has 4.6 million views. It was major for me to be in that video and talking on it. I have actually earned business from people because of this video that I had with Grant. A few weeks ago, my sons and I recorded a video where my son Jordan said that he wanted to meet Grant for his 7th birthday. I sent it to Grant, and he watched it and sent it to his assistant that ended up giving me an appointment for us to go to Miami to meet him. So we went to Miami to meet Grant and Johnny. The camera guy did the video that same day, and on Facebook, the video has 76.9k views, on YouTube 11k views, and on Instagram 41k views which is a total of 128,900 plus views. All of these happened as a result of me pursuing Grant like crazy. But to me, it's absolutely normal because I know the incredible results that they produce for me.

I'm telling you these stories because I've pursued these precious mentors' relationships that I have created because I know how to pursue the mentor. Many people will never get answers to life because they are waiting for the mentor to pick them. I want you to understand that the mentor will never choose you, he doesn't even know you exist. I need for you to identify who you want to learn from and chase them because your future depends on it, because it does.

When I learned that mentorship was the bridge to my future, my life became easier; not easy, just a bit easier, because I now had answers to my problems. The scariest thing, in my opinion, is to have questions and not know where to find the answers. But it's a blessing to have the answers to your problems, and you are no longer living in the land of the unknown.

Let me give you an example of the POWER of mentorship. One day, I was in New Orleans with my mother in a store, and she was looking for some item, and instead of asking an employee exactly where the item was, she went on her own assumption looking for the item and burned 20 minutes searching. I just sat there watching her lose time because she refused to ask. Thank God she finally found it.

I don't want to search; I want to find. I prefer to ask a question so I can redeem time instead of losing time. Time matters to me in a major way; I'm obsessed with the value of time.

That story with my mom showed me how people prefer to play the guessing game in life. I don't want to guess; I want to know the answers so I can execute what the mentor has taught me. Because, as Dr. Murdock has taught me, until you ask a question, your knowledge is accidental, which means you will learn by accident and not on purpose. That's scary to me; I'm too serious about my life to learn by accident.

And that's the value of pursuing the mentor.

Pursue : Follow (someone or something) in order to catch or attack them.

That's what you must be willing to do.

5. I Learned How To Master My Mind

In an attempt for you to understand this section, I must tell you a very extreme story of my life, because it was through this valley of the shadow of death that I learned this. In 2013, I went to Israel for 13 days. I completely enjoyed myself, and I had an incredible time.

Well, the day it was time to leave, I discovered that I didn't have my residence card. Because I'm not an American citizen, I'm a legal residence here in America[CG3] . So here I am, out of the 25 people that went on the trip, and I'm the only guy that was stuck in Israel, across the world which is a 10-hour flight. I promise you I was terrified because in my mind I had no idea what to do. They were kind enough to allow me to get in touch with the pastor that I went on the trip with. He gave me our tour guide's cell number and I called him and told him what happened. He told me that he would call the hotel that I was staying at and tell them to allow me to stay and bring me to the US embassy in the morning.

I got to the hotel. It was the worst sleep I ever had in my life because I knew I was stuck overseas in Israel. I got to the embassy and they told me they couldn't allow me to leave because my name had a record in America, so they said they had to dig more into my name before they just allow me to leave.

They finally allowed me to leave. I landed in New York, and while going through customs, they asked me to come with them. They took me to the immigration office, although I had no idea where they were taking me. They held me in there for over four hours, and the whole time I was lost because I had no idea of the danger I was in.

They finally released me and told me that I had a court day in Houston. I thought nothing of it because I have been to court plenty of times and just showed up and it's over before you know it. The day came for me to go to court, and while I was in the office which was supposed to be a court, the man looked at me and said in the middle of his conversation, "We are detaining you today Mr. Simmons." I stopped and asked him, "Detaining?" He said, "Yes sir."

The detainment lasted 121 days in an immigration jail in Conroe, Texas, which is north of Houston. I was in this place, so lost and heartbroken because I had no idea why I was inside of an immigration jail. I was not here in this country illegally, and every last person there entered this country illegally, so I was really lost. I promise you I cried at least 110 of those 121 days.

Now let me explain to you why I was there. In 2005, while living in New Orleans before Hurricane Katrina, I was placed on probation. When Katrina happened in August 2005, I moved to Houston and never moved back. I really forgot all about it. In my mind, I had a brand new lease on life, so I thought. So what happened while in New York that came up in their system? They saw my American record and looked at me like I was on the run and I was just being busted from running. Because of the probation over a $5 bag of weed, I was in this immigration jail for 121 days.

My mom spent $6,000 because of me being in there for a $5 bag of weed.

Now while I was there, I was depressed because when I was on the streets, I never did time before in my life. The most time I ever did in jail was no more than 24 hours. I can honestly say I've been to jail 5 times, and each time the most I did was 24 hours, and that was when I was really acting up, and thank God it was always super simple stuff.

Now that I'm walking and serving God, I landed in an immigration jail for 121 days; I was confused, my mind was in the fight of my life. My mind was all over the place, and this was the place God taught me how to master my mind.

What in the world does this story have to do with entrepreneurship? Everything! Give me a few more minutes; I'm going to get there soon. This is the story from the Bible that taught me how to Master My Mind.

1 Samuel 17:34-37: But David said to Saul, "Your servant used to keep his father's sheep, and when a lion or a bear came and took a lamb out of the flock, I went out after it and struck it, and delivered the lamb from its mouth; and when it arose against me, I caught it by its beard, and struck and killed it. Your servant has killed both lion and bear; and this uncircumcised Philistine will be like one of them, seeing he has defied the armies of the living God." Moreover David said, "The Lord, who delivered me from the paw of the lion and from the paw of the bear, He will deliver me from the hand of this Philistine."

This is the infamous David and Goliath story. Right here between verses 34-37 David comes to a soon to be battle and hears that Goliath wants to fight the Israelites, but everybody, including King Saul, is terrified. So David tells King Saul, I can kill him. Everybody, including King Saul, looks at him in complete disbelief and like he's crazy. For one, David is a kid probably under 17 years old and Goliath is a real Giant in real life. But then David said something that forever changed my life.

1 Samuel 17:36-37: Your servant has killed both lion and bear; and this uncircumcised Philistine will be like one of them, seeing he has defied the armies of the living God." Moreover David said, "The Lord, who delivered me from the paw of the lion and from the paw of the bear, He will deliver me from the hand of this Philistine."

This is what I called Memorization[CG4] !

David reminded himself of past victories that he had in order to see himself killing Goliath as well. If you noticed, the word in this story is killed, meaning past tense. See, in Entrepreneurship, I promise you a lot of plans are on hold because of your past failures, and you haven't identified that it's your memory reminding you of a perverted past in your life to keep you enslaved to that past.

Not knowing, the past is destroying your future more than you know. David also compared Goliath to some lions and bears which means he saw the giant as the same problem. He didn't see size. Instead, he saw that he was more than able to destroy this enemy.

You have to look at your new enemy on the same level that you saw your past enemy. When you look back on your life, the past enemy looks like an ant today. Well, now you must use your memorization to help you in your present battle. This insight helped me understand that whenever my mind is showing me memories of my past that are fearful, it's automatically the devil trying to enslave me to keep me trapped where I am and scared to move my feet.

Your mind reminds you that the last time you invested $1,000 in this idea it flopped; you never made your money back plus your wife remembers it also, so better not try another stupid idea you had while watching TV, or on the treadmill or wherever you got the idea. At that very second, you have to grab your memorization and intentionally remind yourself of a victory to focus on to get your faith level to where it needs to be so that you get back in the hunt and actually get what you are hunting for.

VISUALIZATION[CG5]

The next step in mastering your mind is visualization. This is also another function of the mind. Memorization focuses on your past, but visualization focuses on your future. Visualization shows you a commercial in your mind of everything going wrong before you even start. It shows you when you post your new t-shirt line that not one person will like your post and they will completely ignore you.

Tell me if you can relate to this analogy. Visualization tells me, "Boy, you crazy if you rent that conference room for $500, no one wants to hear you teach that crazy entrepreneurship stuff, you're even crazier if you think they are going to cancel everything they are doing and spend money with you, you are not Daymond John or Tony Robbins, nobody even like you." Your stomach sometimes hangs over your belt when you wear your suit; you don't look like Terrance J in a suit. Lol. Crazy, right? But this really goes through my mind. It's scary to know that these are real thoughts I have. But notice, it's all future.

Back to David's story. In this same story, both keys are revealed and applied.

1 Samuel 17:46-47:This day the Lord will deliver you into my hand, and I will strike you and take your head from you. And this day I will give the carcasses of the camp of the Philistines to the birds of the air and the wild beasts of the earth, that all the earth may know that there is a God in Israel. Then all this assembly shall know that the Lord does not save with sword and spear; for the battle is the Lord's, and He will give you into our hands."

The first thing David says to Goliath is, "I will kill you today." Future. Then we know that he then kills him. But he first killed him in his mind before he killed him in real life. Because according to the Bible, Goliath didn't die until verse 50.

1 Samuel 17:50-51:So David prevailed over the Philistine with a sling and a stone, and struck the Philistine and killed him. But there was no sword in the hand of David. Therefore David ran and stood over the Philistine, took his sword and drew it out of its sheath and killed him, and cut off his head with it. And when the Philistines saw that their champion was dead, they fled.

We see here, Goliath didn't die until verse 50, but David killed him in his mind first, because and only because, David's mind was trained to think like a winner. This story helped me understand that the devil was after my mind while in this immigration jail, and if it mastered my mind, then my mind would torment me with all kinds of perverted images.

There you have it. I learned to Master Mind. I have a lesson called Mental Toughness 4 Success where I share more insight on this subject plus share the other three keys to Mastering Your Mind. The mind is the greatest tool we have in this life, and very few people learn to Master their Mind. Why do people jump off buildings because of fear, stress, and fear of lack of money? The mind destroyed them.

As an entrepreneur, your mind is being challenged every single day. Every day you have the option to allow memorization or visualization to assist you in accomplishing your goals or surrendering to fear and just act like the dream never existed. The mind is crucial my friend, and I pray you learn to master it.

List 3 things to become a better learner?

1. _____
   _____
   _____
   _____

2. _____
   _____
   _____
   _____

3. _____
   _____
   _____
   _____

CHAPTER 11

BECOME AN OBSESSIVE STUDENT (STUDIER)

This chapter is massively important to every entrepreneur. The average entrepreneur loves their work, loves what they sell, but, I must admit, it takes a true obsession to study what you do. Studying and learning are two completely different tasks. To learn means to accumulate information, to study means to invest hours in truly digesting and comprehending this information.

Study: The devotion of time and attention to acquiring knowledge on an academic subject, especially by means of books.

This definition is super deep. Let's look at the word at the beginning of this definition. To devote endless amount of time. When I think of studying, I think of the great Peyton Manning. To me, Peyton Manning was the first to actually demonstrate the power and benefit of what studying can do for you after investing time into your skill.

Peyton Manning was the first quarterback (I think) to change the play at the line of scrimmage. Meaning the coach called one play and he would change it once he saw the setup of the defense. If you know anything about football, that's extremely dangerous for the coach because when the team loses, the QB never gets the blame for the quarterback mistakes. But because the coaches knew how much he was devoted to his skill, they trusted him. This man changed the game with this approach because it showed the football world the power of the mental side of the game.

This man studied his opponent like no one ever did. He would get to the line with a passing play and notice the defense in a passing coverage and change it to a running play and made an easy 15-yard play. It was insane to see this man use his mind power in the game that enhanced his natural skill with his ability to throw the ball.

But that stemmed from his devotion of time.

Devotion: Love, loyalty, or enthusiasm for a person, activity, or cause.

I like the word loyalty here because it means commitment in all seasons and phases of your life, even in business. It's like the marriage vows, for better or for worst, for rich or for poor, through sickness and in health. Loyalty. Can you say you have been showing loyal devotion through studying in your business? If not, I promise you, if you start, you will find all kinds of hole and leaks that can be fixed in your business and you will find money and opportunities to create more business and expand your business.

I know that to devote time to study might be tough, but also confessing that you don't have time is also an excuse, because we know people make time for what's important. When I first met my wife and told her I was interested, and I wanted more than just a friendship, she told me, "Based on how much you have going on, it seems like you don't have time for a relationship." My words to her were, "I know how to make time for what's important." That was my way of putting my words on the altar for her to hold me accountable to allow her to give me the time to prove my level of interest by devoting time.

3 BENEFITS OF STUDYING (DEVOTING TIME)

1. Accumulation

The word accumulation means a mass or quantity of something that has gradually gathered or been acquired. To gather a wide massive database of information on something.

I'm pretty sure that Peyton Manning invested hours on the computer and watching films, not just one hour. This guy had invested so much he knew every defense because he had seen it all. So nothing really caught him by surprise because he had invested in it all. When you accumulate knowledge, you know what people are going to say before they say it, you can predict word for word on why they can't buy your product or service. Training allows you to know where you are in the conversation and how to handle the situation correctly.

The story I told you about the lady in the learning chapter was a result of studying, not just learning. See, I don't watch one video on a subject, I watch the same video 40 times. Some weeks I watch the same videos seven days straight without fail... why? I already know what the video is going to say by now. I can quote it word for word. I watch it to accumulate, to know it inside out, to get it on the inside so deep that no devil in hell can snatch it away. When we were in school, we knew algebra, geometry, and everything else, but 99% of us don't know it anymore, not because we didn't know it at one time, but because we stopped accumulating, we stopped studying, so it eventually left us as if we never knew it. That's crazy, but those are the pros and cons of abandoning devoting time to accumulate knowledge.

2. You become a master because you have trained.

The difference between a student and a master is the amount of time they have each invested in something, and the results. The results are a byproduct of the time invested. The bodybuilder didn't start benching 500 lbs out of nowhere; he trained. I came to the realization a few weeks ago that at this point in my career, I'm not reading, training, or studying for the sake of being an ocean of knowledge. I'm doing it to keep the knowledge in front of my eyes so that it won't ever leave me.

Proverbs 19:27: Cease listening to instruction, my son. And you will stray from the words of knowledge.

When you cease, which means to stop, you begin to stray. That's just like the kid who leaves his parents' house and moves on his own or goes to college, he slowly began to stray from those words of wisdom and guidance.

When I think of training to be a master, my mind instantly asks myself, how great do you really want to be? Whatever my answer is, then that's what I must be willing to do and train and never cease to devote time to what I claim I want to master.

Training: The action of undertaking a course of exercise and diet in preparation for a sporting event.

synonyms: exercise, exercises, working out, conditioning;

Training is important for you to develop your skills, whether you are preparing in your speaking ability, video editing skills, selling skills, learning how to handle objections, your negotiating skills, or learning how to handle any conversation on any level. Training prepares you for the opportunities. The last thing you want in life is to get opportunities that you haven't prepared for. The mature prepares knowing the moment will come, and when it comes, they maximize the moment.

Like when David killed Goliath, David killed this guy with a slingshot by hitting him on the head with a rock. How much training do you think that took? Basically, a moment was created for him to show his skill, he won the moment, but how many people receive moments that they are not ready for?

Yesterday I was in a conversation with a friend who is starting her nonprofit. I began to tell her that if she wants to have a successful nonprofit, she has to learn how to sell and also how to speak. Every time she asked a question, I showed her the chapters in this book, why this book is necessary, and that I write it because it is going to solve a major problem.

But the reason it is important that she learns to sell is, because to me, running a nonprofit is you making calls and setting appointments trying to sell people on buying into your vision. That's a sales job in my eyes. But it takes training to be ready to sell the vision of that nonprofit. And, of course, you must learn to speak because you will always be in presentation mode, always. So to even succeed in being a nonprofit, you must train, and to train you must be committed to devoting time.

Internalization: Make (attitudes or behavior) part of one's nature by learning or unconscious assimilation.

When you begin to internalize through studying your skill, you begin to see how you can maximize every single opportunity, because this thing is so crystal clear to you that you see nothing else.

Every single day, before I get out of my car to sell my products, I take time while driving to internalize the sell before I make the sale. Before I go and do a presentation, I see it before it happens. When you study your work with obsession, this thing becomes your natural behavior without you even trying. A few weeks ago, my wife and I were at someone's house, and when we walked in, she began to introduce me to the people. As I was shaking everyone's hand, I introduced myself as JJSimmons. I never introduce myself by my first name. It doesn't matter who it is; it can be a person or situation that has nothing to do with business, just like this moment, this was family to her. I still said, "Hey, my name is JJSimmons." A few weeks later when we had a minor argument, she brought that up and told me she didn't like the way I introduced myself. She said I had my business hat on and that wasn't the moment for that. I can admit that I understood her point of view, but to me, I'm so saturated in this JJSimmons brand that the image behind this brand has become the new me and also the real me.

This mentality of me seeing myself as I want to be seen is so deep on the inside that I don't know how to cut it off and at the same time have no interest in turning it off. I'm not an actor that has a British accent, but when I do an American film, I can completely change my accent; this is the real me. But all of this has come as a result of devoting time. Everything that you are today, you first became within.

Let's look at the definition again.

Internalization:Make (attitudes or behavior) part of one's nature by learning or unconscious assimilation.

When looking at this definition with a closer look, it shows me you have brought into what you see within and because of that, it causes an attitude transformation. With that being understood, now I can appreciate people that are committed to their vision to the point where nothing else is important to them because they are fully committed to what they see and also are committed to how they see themselves getting there.

Joshua 1:8 says:This Book of the Law shall not depart from your mouth, but you shall meditate in it day and night, that you may observe to do according to all that is written in it. For then you will make your way prosperous, and then you will have good success.

This Scripture reveals two great secrets to understand. This is probably one of the greatest success Scriptures in the Bible, and this is why.

1. God tells Joshua to Meditate in his Word.
2. After he meditates[CG6] , God promises him that then he will have good success.

Now, please, understand this meditation, which means to ponder on a thought so that you can visualize that thought becoming a reality in your life. But also notice that God is telling Joshua, before you get good success, you must meditate because meditation is going to allow you internalize it first because it has to be in you and deep within you so I can't uproot it from you. Many people know all the principles of success, but very few have internalized the principles, and that's where the miracles are, when it's in your heart not just in your head.

3.   Studying produces transformation

Transformation: A thorough or dramatic change in form or appearance.

I remember one day God began to deal very strongly with me about me dressing professionally to change my appearance. I must admit, it was rough for me because I hated wearing suits; but, I eventually did. But while I was becoming a brand new person within, it was time that my external matched my internal.

Transformation is basically a byproduct of what's taking place within. Studying this thing called entrepreneurship demands change constantly. I heard someone say before that many people never make it in life because when they start to succeed, they stay the same. Staying the same can really hurt your growth because you should always be evolving. Family and close friends want you to stay the same. No, you must become a brand new person daily. Remember, transformation is a dramatic change in form or appearance. Your change should be visible. Your change is official when people who you know that know you can't even recognize you.

Let's go back to the legend, Peyton Manning. He played in 266 games in the NFL. Can you imagine how much studies he had to invest in studying his opponent? But the greatest advantage for him is that he knew almost everything he needed to know about them. After seeing so many teams and so many defenses, you pretty much know their strengths and also their weaknesses. But because of the study time invested, you become almost superhuman to the opponent; they can barely recognize you because your transformation becomes almost unbearable to most.

Do you think Peyton was born superior? No, no one is... but he participated in his ability to become great. He was just willing to study more than the next quarterback, and that's what allowed him to surpass so many.

Study + Devotion Of Time = Accumulation, Mastery, Transformation

List 3 things to become a better obseesive student (studier)?

1. _____
   _____
   _____
   _____

2. _____
   _____
   _____
   _____

3. _____
   _____
   _____
   _____

CHAPTER 12

BECOME A FINISHER

Becoming a finisher is so important to your entrepreneurship journey on so many levels. I want you to be honest with yourself and ask yourself how many projects you have unfinished right now? And then be honest with yourself about how much it haunts you.

It's impossible to escape the convictions that come with it because you will begin to feel like a fraud; at least I do. Because it is really the truth, if you give up on one thing, you can give up on anything. I still remember the day when I walked out of football practice in high school because I was in extreme hamstring pain, and instead of me being honest with the coach, I decided to just leave and go home. I walked out of the back fence when no one was looking and went home. I still remember that at 33 years old. why? I believe because I didn't finish what I started. Think about that, I was probably 15-17 years old, and 18 years later I still remember. I have a memory of me failing, not finishing. Unbelievable!

3 REASONS WHY YOU MUST LEARN TO FINISH

1. You Feel Accomplished

Proverbs 13:19: A desire accomplished is sweet to the soul.

This Scripture truly helps me become determined to finish because it taught me that finishing makes me feel accomplished, so I became obsessed with seeking fulfillment in me finishing. I'm always seeking ways to complete what I started. A few weeks ago, I was invited to do a podcast by a great guy named Pop Darby, so I went to get interviewed. After the interview was done, the host of the show asked me if I would be interested in having my own show. I said, of course, let's work something out where we can meet and discuss exactly what's going on. While being interviewed, they had another person there being interviewed the same day; a young lady named Armani who happened to be a model/actor, and I asked Pop if Armani could be a Co-Host and we three do it together, he said of course. All this happened within 24 hours. I spoke to both of them, and I suggested that we meet the next day. We met and decided that this was what we all wanted to do and now it's official.

But I said all that to say that I move with so much speed because I'm always in pursuit of fulfillment. I'm addicted to it because I have learned that it's sweet to my soul. It allows me to attack the next goal with full confidence. Most people struggle with accomplishing goals not because they don't have what it takes, they struggle because in their mind they know that they give up so much that from the beginning they don't know if they have the gas to see it all the way through.

ACCOMPLISHMENT

1. Something that has been achieved successfully.

2. The successful achievement of a task.

3. An activity that a person can do well, typically as a result of study or practice.

This is what you want; you want to feel accomplished so you can attack the next thing with complete knowing that you will see it through.

When I finished my 1st book, Principle, Participation, Promise, I felt so accomplished that I was in complete bliss for at least one week. Then after that, I knew within me that I had to start writing this book because for one I want to keep building momentum and I wanted to seek that bliss again and again. Right after this book is completed, I will start my next book which is called, My Passion is on steroids. Why? I'm always seeking accomplishment because I have now learned it's very important to my daily success and that will eventually transition to my overall success.

2. It Allows You To Trace

When you complete something, and you feel accomplished, it's a great thing, but the experience in the journey allows you to look back and identify what you did to get there. So now you can look back and repeat the process by tracing what you did. If losing 30 lbs happened because of walking every day for 45 minutes in the morning, drinking 5 smoothies per day, and eating 2 tuna salads every day, you can now look back and trace the process whenever you feel like it. I once heard a millionaire say, "I might can't draw, but I can trace."

When most teams want to beat another team, and they are studying the film on that team, they go to the game where they were beaten by another team because they want to attempt to trace/duplicate what was done by that team. Finishing is the greatest habit you can develop in your life because very few people do it.

Remember what Proverbs 13:19 said, "That a desire accomplished is sweet to the soul." Your level of satisfaction is determined by your habit of becoming a consistent finisher. When I finished my first book, it took me two years. Now that I know what kind of motivation I need, I know what not to do, but now I'm creating a new habit to trace that will become my new normal. As of today, as I'm writing this, I'm on my 30th day of writing this book. I'm completely obsessed with the thought of finishing for many reasons; one, to keep feeling motivated, feeling accomplished, moving to the next goal, maximizing time, knowing that I can, to live an excuse-free life, for feeling good about myself and knowing that I have more potential to keep producing, and the list goes on and on.

3. You Become Your Own Hero

One of the greatest joys of life is when you see yourself in the greatest light ever. I have come to the knowledge that finishing a task, closing the deal, and putting a check next to the checklist does something to your confidence that almost nothing else can do. Based on my own experience, the only way my faith and confidence grows is when I'm crushing it, I'm being a superhuman and anything becomes possible. When you have 75 things undone on your vision board, goal list or whatever it is that you call it, your confidence in you becomes super low. Today is May 27, 2018, and my first book drops this Friday, June 1, 2018, and right now my perception of me is sky high buddy. I'm on fire right now, my faith is on one thousand right not[CG7] , and the benefit of that is me becoming my own hero. Your faith in you is everything. You can only second guess your potential and possibilities when you don't believe in you. It's crazy how most people have faith in other people and what they can do, more than they do themselves. One of the reasons is because they have not become their own heroes in life.

My dear reader, in this entrepreneurship journey, you must become a finisher because the last thing that you want is having a billion ideas that started and were never completed. Make a decision to finish before you get started.

List 3 things to become a better finisher?

1. _____
   _____
   _____
   _____

2. _____
   _____
   _____
   _____

3. _____
   _____
   _____
   _____

CHAPTER 13

BECOME A CREATOR

In 2016, I created a T-shirt that says, Entrepreneurs Lives Matter. Before I created that shirt, for almost two months before that I was sad, worried, I would even say depressed, and what was even worse about it is, I didn't know. For days, I thought I was having a devil problem; meaning, I thought I was under heavy attack from evil forces. Then one day, the heavens opened wide for me and gave me the beginning stages of one of the greatest revelations of my life.

The day before I created Entrepreneur Lives Matter, I was sad. Even while I was printing the shirts, I was a bit sad. The next day, I woke up in complete overflowing joy and was so surprised and completely off guard because I remembered that I was depressed the day before. A few minutes later, I was reminded that when God created the world, whenever he created something he looked at it and said it is good.

Genesis 1:1-31:

10 And God called the dry land Earth, and the gathering together of the waters He called Seas. And God saw that it was good

12 And the earth brought forth grass, the herb that yields seed according to its kind, and the tree that yields fruit, whose seed is in itself according to its kind. And God saw that it was good.

17 God set them in the firmament of the heavens to give light on the earth, 18 and to rule over the day and over the night, and to divide the light from the darkness. And God saw that it was good.

25 And God made the beast of the earth according to its kind, cattle according to its kind, and everything that creeps on the earth according to its kind. And God saw that it was good.

31 Then God saw everything that He had made, and indeed it was very good.

Notice each one of these verses ends with God saying that what He created is good. And verse 31 says that God said that everything He created was very good.

What I learned was that because He created something from nothing, when He looked at His creation, He found pleasure in His creation and because of that He said it is good. With that knowledge, what I learned was because I created that shirt, I found extreme pleasure in my creation, and that was the reason for my joy. Because of that experience, I'm writing this chapter to you today. And I believe that without this extra chapter, this book is a complete half done job. Being a creator is extremely key to your growth, you can't grow without creating and creating frequently.

5 REASONS YOU MUST BECOME A CREATOR

1. Creating Creates New Income

Yesterday I went into this barber shop and showed the barber my book, and they were so amazed and purchased my book with no hesitation. They were so excited for me and my new creation that they spent money quickly. These guys have bought my shirts before but because I created something new they purchased something new that I created.

Creation is important because it allows you to have multiple products and multiple services that people can find interest in which is important. Even though Walmart didn't create all the products in their store, we see that they don't rely on one product and because of that, we spend money on something because the selection is so optional.

A few years ago, Coca-Cola was losing a lot of money from their competitor Pepsi, and they were extremely worried, so they did something really brilliant. They had a meeting and decided to create Dasani water, Minute Maid Juice, they brought Zico Coconut water, and a few other brands. The reason they did that was because they figured they weren't about to go into a battle of Coca-Cola vs. Pepsi, but, they would create brands that people were drinking on a regular basis, which is the same reason Google brought YouTube. Creation allows you to attract new eyeballs, which in turn creates income.

2. Creation Creates New Followers

Creation is everything to your growth. In 2017, I did my first conference in New Orleans. This was completely challenging to me because even though I'm from New Orleans, I knew I had to get people in the chairs. I knew that my neighborhood friends weren't going to come because most of them don't live in New Orleans anymore and the rest that live there are in different worlds.

But I put my money into this event by faith knowing that this is what I needed to do to prove it to myself that I can conquer new territory. I needed to do it to show my New Orleans family that my gift is more profound than just listening to me on audio. I needed to do it to challenge myself to expand. It was a must do for me. When I did this event, people came, but in the process, I created new relationships with new people who still follow my movement and buy products from me to this day. It expanded my audience, but that was only a result of me being intentional about creating.

Today, every decision I make is for the sake of growth. If it doesn't create growth in my life, I'm not interested. I have discovered that the quickest way to grow is to add problems to your life on purpose so that you can solve them on purpose. Let me explain.

My first book just dropped June 1st, as I write this book it's June 2nd. The whole month of June, I will be in New Orleans promoting my new book. But every Sunday and Monday of June, I will be back in Houston to do the podcast that I have already committed to.

So imagine me doing all that traveling going back and forth to New Orleans and Houston every week and I just decided to add something more to my list. I have just decided to add my book release party which I'm shooting to do July 7th. Based on common sense alone, it doesn't make sense for me to add another thing to my list because I know how much effort it takes to pull this off.

But I also know from a negative side that if I don't do it, I'm not challenging myself to become all that I can be and see all that I can see. To create this book release party will only grow me, it's impossible for it to damage me, it will only enhance what I'm already doing.

In this season of my life, I completely understand how important it is that a multitude of people are aware of my business and services. Because of that, I'm always promoting, always planning on new ways to create new followers. The more people are familiar with me, the greater my chances are of people buying from me.

Let's assume you live in Orange, Texas, and you are well known in Orange, and you just refuse to leave your beloved city in Texas. Guess what? Just in case you don't know, your income and expansion is limited to your lack of drive to want to be known in other places as well. What I learned is that if they love me in New Orleans, Beaumont, Atlanta, Miami, Houston, and Dallas, most likely they will love me in Chicago as well. But it's my responsibility to go and make myself known to these people.

One of the reasons why creating creates new followers is because not everybody is just interested in one thing that you do. I'm really not interested in Chic-fia-l[CG1] chicken sandwich, I have never bought one, but I buy those salads every time, and because that is an option for me I buy that, but it also makes me a follower of the brand.

I want you to adopt this new way of thinking to your mindset. Right now I only have five different products that I sell. Everybody that follows my movement came through one of these channels. So as a student of my business, I'm always planning on how to create more ways that will attract new people to my business.

I'm not satisfied with just 20,000 people knowing me, I want 20 million, but I also know that if I reach 20 million people, I must keep creating new things to attract another 20 million people because everyone is not interested in the same things. I want you to sit down and make a plan on what you must do to attract new people to you because they are out there just waiting for you to create something they are interested in to latch on to you.

The people that come to my seminars would probably never buy a book. The people that read my books would probably never buy coaching from me because they feel like I can watch him for free online or just buy a book. The people that buy coaching would probably never buy my books because they are just not readers, and I know that, and because of that, I'm always planning on new and improved ways to create to keep attracting. And that, my friend, is why you must continue to create and become addicted to creating.

3. Creation Makes Productivity Your New Normal

When you tap into your God nature as a creator, you will discover that all this time you had potential that was untapped. I promise that is a frustrating thing to have because you realize it just reveals all the time that you have wasted.

But on the flip side, it motivates you like never before. When you fall in love with the creator in you, you become addicted to creation. Right now, I'm so motivated to finish this book, not to see this book in other people's hand. I'm motivated to write the next book, and the next, and then the next.

For you to make productivity your new normal, you must place daily a high demand on your productivity. For you to stay productive, you must hold yourself accountable daily and be extremely rough on yourself and produce everything you see in your head that you were created to be.

4. Creation Allows You to Experience the God Within You.

One of the greatest things I have learned is that creation has a voice, and that voice is always encouraging you to be great, be amazing, be extraordinary. The problem with this is that even though that voice is always speaking, we have a choice to obey or not. Very few decide to obey that voice and because they don't obey, very few get to experience how truly amazing they can be or even greater they can BECOME.

When I receive testimonies of people who have read my book, my ears really don't hear the testimony at first. I normally always say to myself wow, I'm so glad I wrote this book because I had someone answer in my heart, but if it were not created, this, their problem would still be unanswered.

I was in Beaumont, Texas in 2013, and a guy bought an audio program from me; I didn't think much about it after he gave me the money because I have sold thousands of CDs. But around 6 pm, I received a call from him, and he was in tears, and as I attempted to talk to him, he said, "Bro, the sermon on this CD answered a problem that I have been having for the last three years in my life."

He then went on to tell me how at first he didn't want to buy it because I was black and he was white, and just began to explain that he is not a racist, but it's sad how our natures sometimes make us judge people for no reason. But he was just so grateful he bought it that day. This guy and I are still friends to this day, and it's so amazing to remember that my creation gave him direction for his life. It's so priceless.

5. Lack of Creation Causes Decay.

At the beginning of this chapter, I told the story of my Entrepreneurs Lives Matter T-shirt. Before I actually created the shirts, I had the idea for months, and I know that my depression was because of my delay in pursuing the idea. My sadness was self-created because of my slowness to create.

So many people today are sad and depressed because they are not creating. You talk to anyone who loves painting, fixing cars, writing, whatever they love, I promise you if they are not creating, they are not happy with themselves for abandoning that talent. The most painful feeling in the world is ignoring your talent and allowing it to decay within you.

In my opinion, that is irresponsible because God created you to create, so in return, we can equip the next person to create.

List 3 things to become a better negotitator?

1. _____
   _____
   _____
   _____

2. _____
   _____
   _____
   _____
   _____

3. _____
   _____
   _____
   _____
   _____

CHAPTER 14

BECOME AN OPPORTUNIST

LOOK FOR OPPORTUNITIES!

When the average person thinks of the word opportunities, they think of money, which is part of the problem. For that reason, we get so little results in our lives and businesses.

A few months ago, Grant Cardone was in his Instagram account showing that he was flying out to Houston from Miami. When I saw that, I immediately reached to his wife Elena to see if she would send the location of where they would be. Thank God she did.[FB2] When I arrived there, they were already leaving the restaurant at that second. It was such an awesome moment. All I was trying to do was do an interview on Grant. I was not expecting all that has come out of that opportunity. Three things have happened because of that opportunity. The first was I blessed with the opportunity to interview Grant. The second thing was, Grant's camera team took a clip from that day and created a video that's called Who is Grant Cardone that at this moment has 4.7 Million views that I'm in. 4.7 Million people have heard my voice and seen my face just because I was looking for an opportunity. The third thing that happened was, the whole time I pulled up on them at the restaurant, his camera person named Johnny was recording the whole deal. A few weeks ago, the media team created a video called Grant Cardone walking up the street that I happened to be in the whole video. The day this video got uploaded, it had 12k views in 24 hours which as of today has 16k views.

My Instagram was on fire that day, and I had no idea why so many people were sending me DMs. Later that night, I discovered why so many people were messaging me. Now, remember I was just looking for opportunities and because of my pursuit I have been blessed with the opportunity to be seen by almost 4.7 million by just simply reaching out to Elena Cardone and her replying because I was looking for opportunity.

LEARN TO CREATE OPPORTUNITIES

I mentioned all throughout this book about my t-shirt line that I have created for entrepreneurs. In 2015, I created the t-shirt that says #selfemployed. Now, being an opportunist, that shirt was created on purpose. Why? Because years ago, I learned that the quickest way to make money is to study where money is already flowing and just tap into the flow and money will come my way.

For example, every gas station in the world sells coffee today. Why? Because millions of Americans today are buying coffee every morning. So one day the gas stations decided to get very focused on their coffee products. Dunkin donuts, McDonald's, and other companies started to pay close attention to this income stream. But my point is, they saw an opportunity and decided to maximize that opportunity.

I did the same thing; I saw plenty of money flowing to Entrepreneurship products, so I created one. My t-shirts were me being an opportunist. Many people will never admit that, but I am. There is nothing wrong with being an opportunist. In today's economy, some people are selling products that they could care less for, but they do because they saw a need, so they decided to start selling that product.

Look at it this way, the fast food industry are opportunists because they take advantage of us not cooking, not having time to cook, being lazy, hate cooking, etc. They have made billions maybe even trillions from that knowledge from us. Creating an opportunity is basically you seeing a need and not afraid to capitalize on that need.

Many people see a need that they are scared to fill because of the possible criticism they might receive from outsiders. Learning to create opportunities will train you on how to create crazy productivity in your life to put you in action at all times in your life.

My first book, Principle, Participation, Promise came out June 1st, and by the grace of God, the book has been selling great. So one day, I sat back and said to myself, "I need to create an event too because most of these people will most likely be willing to come and hear me speak. So I quickly created a seminar because as an opportunist, you only have small windows to capitalize.

GIVE OTHERS OPPORTUNITIES

A few days ago, I was in New Orleans working, and I decided to stop by a friend of mine who just started a business selling deserts that name Kd's Nola treats and few other items. My intent was to just go by her place and support her. As much as I'm an opportunist, I was not thinking of myself. Well, as a result, I bought a smoothie which was $7.05, she brought my book for $20, and I gave her a free Self-Employed t-shirt which is $20.

She posted me on her Instagram account which gave me more than 500 views in a 24-hour period. I posted her on my account which probably gave her some views as well. Now, I must admit that her page yielded me more views than mine did for her, but my point is, I was not looking for anything but to support her because I love what she is doing as an Entrepreneur and I had to support her. But because my intent was so pure, we went crazy that day supporting each other; it was truly amazing.

Listen, learn to become an opportunist, everything that is successful today is because someone decided to capitalize on an opportunity.

List 3 things to become a better opportunist?

1. _____
   _____
   _____
   _____

2. _____
   _____
   _____
   _____

3. _____
   _____
   _____
   _____

CHAPTER 15

BECOME A MONSTER

WHY MUST YOU BECOME A MONSTER?

Bulletproof: Designed to resist the penetration of bullets.

In the economy we are living in, you must train your heart and mind to resist shots taken toward you. A few days ago, I had a complete stranger go through my YouTube channel commenting crazy disrespectful things on my page. But thank God I was built for this war I'm in.

You must be designed for this warzone called entrepreneurship. Just in case you didn't know, Bill Gates (Microsoft) and Steve Jobs (Apple) competed in the same times. I know you probably don't understand how extremely tough that is.

Being bulletproof is so important today. Look at how much all the sports news talk about LeBron James. None of these stations would even have news to report if it wasn't for LeBron. In 2017-2018 season, these people talked about every single game of the season. It was so unbelievable to watch how much impact this man has had on sports news.

I remember watching a billionaire tell a story about how journalists would write news articles online and in printed magazines about what they disliked about a company and these companies would change what these journalists would critique about their business. The billionaire was upset because his point was, these journalists never in their lives ran a business before, and here they can criticize companies, and they change their whole business because a complete nobody had an opinion. That's what happens when you are not bulletproof.

You must learn to guard your heart against haters and even fans sometimes. The haters, because if you are not strong enough, their words can wound you and slow you down. The fans, because if you are not careful, their celebration can puff your head up and you start thinking you are untouchable.

In order to be bulletproof, you must understand that people will intentionally take shots at you. And it's your full responsibility to resist those shots fired if you plan on becoming a monster.

The LA Lakers lost one year to the Boston Celtics and Koby Bryant admitted that the Boston Celtics were stronger and more physically dominating. They were not as ready as they thought they were. When you think of the New England Patriots, you think of this imaginary creature, you think of a Monster that is indestructible.

In today's business, who is the imaginary monster who comes to mind? Amazon.

Amazon is a monster. When people think of a startup today, they think of Amazon first because Amazon has created a brand that has frightened almost every business owner. Amazon has completely put so many people out of business that it is extremely unbelievable, but it's happening at the same time. Amazon has taken billions out of Walmart's yearly income. Anytime a company can disrupt Walmart, you know it's not a game.

A few years ago, Kevin Durant went to the Golden State Warriors. The Warriors were already great before he came, but now with him, they have become the Monster of the NBA. The day he went, all hell broke loose in the sports industry. But guess what, Kevin Durant has won two rings since going there and was a dominant reason on why they won. In the midst of winning, the world will take shots; you must know how to ignore and resist shots fired at you. And because of that, The Golden State Warriors are the monster of the NBA at the moment.

So many people have done business with me because of my full-time monster approach. People like dealing with people that are crazy, unreasonable, psycho, and lunatic in the conviction about their business. I promise, if you study everybody that has done amazing things in this world, they were all crazy, psycho in their day to day operations.

I have discovered that the reason people like crazy people is because the crazies demonstrate faith in this faithless world. Everyone is so humble and passive. Very few people these days demonstrate faith; everyone is hiding behind the internet, hiding behind their desk. So when the world finds someone that is taking risk, they fall in love with him or her because this person is demonstrating to them what they know that they should be doing already themselves.

Think about all the people who you admire and then think about why you admire them. I bet any money it is because they demonstrated courage to you and gave you permission to be crazy in your faith. People compliment me all the time for being a beast. When was the last time people called you a beast? People like beasts, people like people that don't disappear in the marketplace. People like people that have the audacity to say, "My product is One Billion Dollars," and you are only selling a 24-ounce glass of water. LOL!

I promise you they do, why? Because it's attractive. Suge Knight made fun of Puffy for dancing in the videos, but look at Puffy now. Sean Combs is a brand that is massive. He didn't disappear; he became a beast, he committed to doing what everyone else was completely afraid of doing and officially mastered it like no other. Listen, my dear reader, you have to become a beast. In this jungle, it's eat or be eaten; it's sell or be sold.

It's easy to decide to have a side hustle and call yourself an entrepreneur, but you must become a beast entrepreneur if you plan on surviving this jungle that has wild beasts in it that wake every day looking for some prey to kill in order for them to eat.

List 3 things to become a better monster?

1. _____
   _____
   _____
   _____

2. _____
   _____
   _____
   _____

3. _____
   _____
   _____
   _____

CHAPTER 16

BECOME A NON-EMOTIONAL SAVAGE

This chapter is probably the most important chapter in this whole book because if your emotional stability is not right, you can't:

Sell
Market
Speak
Negotiate
Focus in order to study
Network

Nothing is possible when your emotions are running crazy on the inside of you. Many people are extremely talented but struggle with their emotions, and unfortunately, that is their disaster. I have layer upon layer that I would like to teach you in this chapter that would equip you to master your emotions.

A few years ago, when my sons were living with their mom, she and I had some disagreement at the time. I went to their house to visit them and she would not let them outside to see me. I drove maybe 20 minutes to come and see them, and when I got there, she wouldn't let me.

I promise you, I went in my car and drove home to north Houston and cried for 45 minutes on my ride.

But that same day, I had a video that I wanted to record, and I jumped out of my car and recorded one of my favorite videos ever. But minutes before that, I was an emotional wreck. What allowed me to do such a thing? Learning how to become an emotional beast.

Years ago, I discovered that in this life, you will have daily problems and if you have no strength over your problems, your problems will cause you so much visible problems that they will cripple you from your productivity and your destiny.

As I write you this at this very second, I'm facing a major problem, but because I live in this revelation of being an emotional savage, I know I'm accountable to myself to work out this revelation of mine that I'm teaching you.

Proverbs 25:28: Whoever has no rule over his own spirit is like a city broken down without walls.

Let me give you some understanding on this Scripture. In biblical times, the walls protected the city from enemies trying to sneak into the cities to attack the people. That's why they have a biblical term called watchmen on the wall. These men's job was to stand on this wall and watch for any strange activity.

So this Scripture is saying when you have no dominance over your spirit, you are like a city that has no protection.

When your emotions have no protection, enemies come and go as they please. When a city has no watchman on guard, any enemy would be able to come and invade the city and completely catch the city off guard and destroy the city because no one was on watch.

This Scripture taught me to dominate my emotions and to always be extra cautious on what I allow to trigger my emotions.

In life, when you are not aware of attacks, you can be in mental warfare but emotionally stable.

Your mind is at war always, and when I say at war, I just don't mean that you are suicidal, I just mean you have a mental activity that has nothing to do with what you are trying to focus on.

This Scripture wants us to rule our spirit.

I had to learn how to ignore my emotional and mental warfare even though it is officially draining me and still function as if nothing is happening. But because I'm so internally motivated, I can still operate because my heart is fixed to be great regardless of circumstances.

This idea that I'm sharing with you might sound completely impossible, but that's the whole reason the name of this chapter is called, become an emotional savage. Meaning you must become emotionally out of touch with reality that you learn how to function in the midst of everything that's happening around you and dominate what's happening within you.

That's the key to learning to dominate what's happening within you because in all honesty, that's all you can control. You can't control what's going on in the world, the news, politics, religion, immigration, etc., you can't control any of that. You can only control your internal.

Again, rule your spirit.

Tap Into Your God Nature.

Matthew 26 36:54: Then Jesus came with them to a place called Gethsemane, and said to the disciples, "Sit here while I go and pray over there." 37 And He took with Him Peter and the two sons of Zebedee, and He began to be sorrowful and deeply distressed. 38 Then He said to them, "My soul is exceedingly sorrowful, even to death. Stay here and watch with Me."

39 He went a little farther and fell on His face, and prayed, saying, "O My Father, if it is possible, let this cup pass from Me; nevertheless, not as I will, but as You will."

40 Then He came to the disciples and found them sleeping, and said to Peter, "What! Could you not watch with Me one hour? 41 Watch and pray, lest you enter into temptation. The spirit indeed is willing, but the flesh is weak."

42 Again, a second time, He went away and prayed, saying, "O My Father,[h]if this cup cannot pass away from Me unless I drink it, Your will be done." 43 And He came and found them asleep again, for their eyes were heavy.

44 So He left them, went away again, and prayed the third time, saying the same words. 45 Then He came to His disciples and said to them, "Are you still sleeping and resting? Behold, the hour [i]is at hand, and the Son of Man is being betrayed into the hands of sinners. 46 Rise, let us be going. See, My betrayer is at hand."

47 And while He was still speaking, behold, Judas, one of the twelve, with a great multitude with swords and clubs, came from the chief priests and elders of the people.

48 Now His betrayer had given them a sign, saying, "Whomever I kiss, He is the One; seize Him." 49 Immediately he went up to Jesus and said, "Greetings, Rabbi!" and kissed Him.

50 But Jesus said to him, "Friend, why have you come?"Then they came and laid hands on Jesus and took Him. 51 And suddenly, one of those who were with Jesus stretched out his hand and drew his sword, struck the servant of the high priest, and cut off his ear.

52 But Jesus said to him, "Put your sword in its place, for all who take the sword will [j]perish by the sword. 53 Or do you think that I cannot now pray to My Father, and He will provide Me with more than twelve legions of angels? 54 How then could the Scriptures be fulfilled, that it must happen thus?"

This story put the ultimate stamp on my life and showed me how to dominate my emotions once and for all..In the Chapter about becoming a learner I told you the story about me facing a immigration case and how in there I had to learn how to master mind

But now let me add more to this same story and how this story from the Jesus being in the garden helped me master my emotions.

They are a few things happening in this story while jesus is in this garden.

He knew he was being betrayed by judas
He was looking to his friends for comfort
his soul was sorrowful Then He said to them, "My soul is exceedingly sorrowful, even to death.
He got arrested

So here I'm in this prison fighting this case not knowing what my future held for me because at this point it was truly uncertain. And two things happen in this story that showed me everything I need to see in order to fight the battles of life an become an emotional savage that I am today.

One minute we see that Jesus is in sorrow in verse 38

Matthew 26:38: Then He said to them,"My soul is exceedingly sorrowful, even to death.

Next thing we see when the people came to arrest him he made a statement that I will forever remember.

Matthew 26:52:53: But Jesus said to him, "Put your sword in its place, for all who take the sword will [j]perish by the sword. Or do you think that I cannot now pray to My Father, and He will provide Me with more than twelve legions of angels?

In verse 38 Jesus is having a emotinal rollercoaster to where he from his own mouth admits that his is soul which is your mind,will,emotions,imagination and your intellect is exceedingly sorrowful,which means he was extremely stressed out to the point it was beyond bearable.

But then in verse 52-53 Jesus transforms his mind to become a super human. Look at his statement he tells Peter 53 Or do you think that I cannot now pray to My Father, and He will provide Me with more than twelve legions of angels?

One minute he is stressed out the next minute he taps back into his divine nature. Please understand this extremely significant truth it doesn't matter how much skill,talent,giftedness you have if your spiritual awarness is not in tact you will fail big time in this life. Many people are homeless today,millions have committed suicide because they never master the emotinal component to being productive and successful in life.

I promise you skill doesn't benefit you when your emotions are not mastered. What Jesus did you must learn to do in order to be successful. You must learn to go from having a major conversation with your spouse about every bill that's due by tommorrow morning,or from leaving your child school and how your child just cant figure it out how to behave regardless of what you try to do for them or give them. And walk into your next meeting with the biggest most geninue smile you have ever had on your face and show all your teeth like absolutely nothing just happen a few minutes ago. Then go and conduct that meeting like a true professional and ask the client for their business of $150k-$10 million like a true monster and be unwavering in your ask.

The biggest pro and con is that you become Non-Emotional for life from this point on for life. Scary but good.

Let me explain.

Its great because you will learn to guard your heart from all sources of unwanted emotions,news,information whatever is coming your way. After a while you will began to become so bulletproof to everything. My wife biggest frustrations with me is anything painful,emotional that had noting to do with us grabs zero of my attention. I don't even try to act like I'm interested because I'm absolutely not.

The down side to becoming a Emotional Savage is you will give off the vibe that nothing outside of your world interest you. Which is actually true in my case. See I have learn that in order for me to be successful is that I have to have laser focus on whats important to me. I cant go around life adopting peoples problem and making them my own. I just cant,because some people will just drop a load on you with no mercy and give you more the very next day. If you entertain everyone's problem and give everyone your time for you to be there counseler you will lose your mind and life in the process.

I have a very core principle to my life.

I rather hurt your feelings,before I hurt mines.

Meaning I prefer to tell you,listen brother I'm really not interested in what you are talking about at the moment I have more important things to tend to at the moment. Than me giving my undivided attention for one hour and listen to all your problems and lose my one hour that I will never get back and in the process not solve your problem also. You have to guard your heart from all the problems this life is so willingly to invite into your world.

List 3 things to become a better non emotional salvage?

1. _____

2. _____

3. _____

CONCLUSION

I would first like to say thank you so much for purchasing and reading the greatest entrepreneurship book written in the last 200 years.

This book in my opinion is a must read for all Entrepreneurs because it is my full conviction that in this economy you must be multiple people in one in order to do business. You must be the chef that knows how to market to your current customers, market to potential customers, and create the customer that the marketing creates for you.

My whole Entrepreneurship journey I have learned that everything you want in life is connected to a skill. Many people refuse to invest the time to develop the correct skill in order to move forward. It's my prayer that inside this book you find what skill you need to attain to further equip you to be what I call a 21st Century Entrepreneur.

Think about the top law firm in your city,they have commercials on Television all day,they have radio commercials,they have billboards all throughout the city. They understand what very few have yet to accept,which is you must become more than what currently are to attract new people to your business.

YOU MUST LEARN TO BECOME

turn into,change into,be transformed into,be converted into

ABOUT THE AUTHOR

J.J. Simmons was born in Honduras in 1984. At the age of three, he moved with his family to New Orleans, where he was raised. When he was twelve years old, he went down the wrong path in life. He started smoking weed and rebelled against his family. At fourteen years old he found Jesus. Amazingly the same streets where he found drugs, he found God. However, he faced a dilemma; the enemy convinced him that he was too young to serve God, so he backslid. Then to the age of twenty he ran from God and the calling on his life. As a consequence, he had six near death experiences. The last two near death experiences were eye opening to J. J. Simmons and got his full attention.

First one that got his attention occurred as he was traveling from Chicago, the train derailed. He felt like the prophet Jonah and felt like he was cursed. He thought perhaps the train derailed because of him. The second experience that got his attention was when he was in a very critical car accident.

Both of these experiences caused him to yield to God and reach his breaking point. He was tired of running from God and decided to get his life right. J.J. Simmons, had some choices he had to make. He was a local hip-hop artist in the Houston. He was traveling and getting a lot of attention. He had a song that played on the radio, Sundays for seventeen consecutive weeks. This resulted in a lot of momentum building up. In addition, he was a television host of a hip hop show every Friday night. Even though J.J. Simmons had a lot going for him, he was tired from running from God. He recommitted his life to Jesus at the age of twentythree. He gave up that hip hop life style.

Ten years later, he is an entrepreneur and does seminars about it. God called him into entrepreneurship. J. J. Simmons is an anointed teacher. He teaches kingdom principles in a simplistic way. Many people have received awesome revelation as they are able to take the principles being taught and execute them. Since he gave up his hip-hop show for God, God gave him a local show called, "Thou Shall Prosper TV" that airs globally seven days per week. The goal of this show is to empower people to remember what Genesis says about being fruitful and multiple, subdue the earth, and have dominion and to prosper. This show encourages people all around the world to operate in their full God nature because God created us in His image and His likeness. J. J. Simmons has been ordained by God to resurrect these principles within the human spirit. His mission is to make sure that God's people are fruitful, multiplying, and living a prosperous life.

Made in the USA
Lexington, KY
20 December 2019